SELLING
BOLDLY

ALEX GOLDFAYN

SELLING
BOLDLY

Applying the New Science of
Positive Psychology
to Dramatically Increase Your
Confidence, Happiness, and Sales

WILEY

Published by John Wiley & Sons, Inc., Hoboken, New Jersey.
Published simultaneously in Canada.

For general information on our other products and services or for technical support, please contact our
Customer Care Department within the United States at (800) 762-2974, outside the United States at
(317) 572-3993, or fax (317) 572-4002.

Wiley publishes in a variety of print and electronic formats and by print-on-demand. Some material
included with standard print versions of this book may not be included in e-books or in
print-on-demand. If this book refers to media such as a CD or DVD that is not included in the
version you purchased, you may download this material at http://booksupport.wiley.com. For more
information about Wiley products, visit www.wiley.com.

Library of Congress Cataloging-in-Publication Data is Available:

ISBN 9781119436331 (Hardback)
ISBN 9781119436348 (ePDF)
ISBN 9781119436355 (ePub)

Cover design: Wiley

Printed in the United States of America

10 9 8 7 6 5 4 3 2 1

For Noah and Bella, who teach me how to live boldly and fearlessly every day.

Contents

About the Author

Alex Goldfayn is the CEO of The Revenue Growth Consultancy, a seven-figure solo consulting practice which adds 10 to 20 percent annual revenue growth to clients by systematically implementing the mindsets and actions in this book, with layers of accountability, recognition, and reward.

Alex engages with organizations over 6 to 24 months to create the right proactive communication habits among customer-facing staff. The *day* Alex's clients launch their Selling Boldly revenue growth actions, they are communicating exponentially more with customers and prospects than they were the day before. And this goes on for years. This is how his clients attain and maintain such dramatic and rapid growth.

Alex does more than 50 speeches and workshops each year, and regularly keynotes large annual association meetings as well as sales kickoff events.

You can learn more about all this work at www.goldfayn.com.

Alex is the author of *The Revenue Growth Habit: The Simple Art of Growing Your Business by 15% in 15 Minutes A Day* (like the book you're reading now, also published by John Wiley & Sons). It was selected as the sales book of the year by 800-CEO-Read, and Forbes selected it as one of the top 15 business books of the year.

He is also the author of *Evangelist Marketing: What Apple, Amazon and Netflix Understand About Their Customers (That Your Company Probably Doesn't)*, published by BenBella Books.

To learn more about growing your sales 10 to 20 percent annually with Alex, or to schedule him to speak at your next event, call him at 847-459-6322 or email him at alex@goldfayn.com.

PART

I

Fear Is the Greatest Enemy of Sales . . . and Positive Psychology Is the Antidote

1

The Single Greatest Killer of Sales

Want to grow sales? Here is an executive summary of this book in two sentences and two steps:

  The first step is to know how good you are so that you gain confidence, positivity, and boldness.

  The second step is to communicate with customers and prospects more, because the more we communicate, the more we sell. (The less we communicate, the less we sell. It never works the other way. We can never communicate less, and sell more.)

That's the book in a nutshell. If you keep reading, you'll learn in deep detail how to dramatically increase your positivity, confidence, and joy by listening to your happy customers—and then, simply, offering to help them more.

That's how easy it is to grow sales.

We begin with three stories that lay out the single greatest killer of sales growth.

The Coffee Shop

I was at the airport in Minneapolis, ordering an iced coffee, and the young woman behind the counter asked me if I would like a bottle of water with that.

This stopped me in my tracks because I teach all of my clients this technique—I call it the did you know question—and although it's an incredibly simple question that requires only a few seconds, almost nobody ever asks a question like this. Anywhere, ever.

I asked her, "Do they teach you to ask this question?"

"Yes, they do," she said. "It's a part of our training."

"How many people buy a bottle of water?"

You know what she said?

"Almost everybody."

Guess how much the water cost? Five dollars!

The coffee?

It cost $3.

It's amazing.

With this simple question, this coffee shop nearly *triples* its sales, from $3 to $8.

With water!

Was I mad at her for trying to sell me a $5 bottle of water?

Of course not. She was trying to help me. And like everybody else she asks, I know that a $5 bottle of water is absurd.

So how was she being helpful?

I was getting on an airplane. I needed water, anyway.

If I didn't buy it from her, in a single transaction, I would have to take my coffee, and my rolling luggage down the terminal to a gift shop and procure my bottle of water. I'd have to set down my luggage, and my coffee, take a water out of the cooler, risk *dropping* my coffee on the floor because I'm now holding both the water and the coffee in one hand, as I try to get to the other, new, checkout line. Once I would get to the front of the line, I would have to set everything down again—luggage, coffee, and water—and pay. Again. And how much money have I saved? A dollar or two? Maybe? I could use that time to relax, or make a proactive phone call to a customer to check in (*much* more on this to come throughout the book).

The young checkout person at the coffee shop offered me water, which (1) saved me time, and (2) allowed me to complete my beverage acquisitions in one transaction. I valued that. I appreciated it. So, apparently, did nearly everybody else she asked. Remember, she asks everybody, and *almost everybody* buys the water.

And so, I ask you: *What is your bottle of water?*

What can you sell to your customers, who have been buying the same products and services from you for years, decades maybe, without considering what else they can buy from you? Right now, today, your customers are buying from the competition products or services they could be buying from you. These are products and services they *should* be buying from you. In fact, your customers *would like to* buy these things from you. After all, they've been with you for all these years for a reason. They're very happy doing business with you. And everybody knows one purchase order is better than two or three or four. They *want* to buy more from you and, of course, you would like to sell them additional products.

But none of that is possible, because they don't know.

We don't tell them what else they can buy.

And they're too busy to know. Or ask. They simply assume they can only buy from us that which they have bought for years. And *we* assume that that is all they need! They niche us, and we niche them.

They would buy, if we would ask. But we do not, so they do not.

In this book, in Chapter 27, I will teach you exactly how to ask your customers to buy *your* bottles of water.

The Insulation Contractor

Several years ago, my family moved into a new home.

We had a room over the garage, and it was colder than the rest of the house.

So I called three insulation companies. I'd never bought insulation services before.

They all came out, did some testing, and sent me their quotes.

I received quotes from all three of them.

But only one of the guys followed up with me *after* he sent the quote.

Guess who got the business?

That's right, the guy who followed up.

Guess who was the most expensive?

Right again, the guy who followed up.

So why did he get the business?

By following up with me, was he bothering me?

Was he annoying me?

Was he taking up my time when he called?

No, none of those things.

When he followed up, he was showing me he cared.

The other guys did the opposite.

When they did not follow up, they were showing me they *did not care*.

But their expensive competitor called me, and emailed me.

He even said to me, "Why don't you send me the other two quotes, and I'll see if I missed anything."

I know this wasn't really fair to the other guys, but they weren't talking to me. In fact, they were nowhere to be found.

I teach my clients a three-step follow-up process that closes 20 percent of all outstanding quotes and proposals! Each follow-up is a one-line email that takes about five seconds to copy and paste. If you replace one of the emails with a phone call, we find that a whopping 30 percent of all outstanding proposals and quotes close. Can you imagine?

The customer asked you for a quote or proposal, and you sent it. *You've done the work!* But when the customer doesn't reply with a quick "yes," we very rarely follow up. By the way, customers will rarely call to say "no," they are not accepting your quote. They feel badly about saying no, and nobody really enjoys rejecting an offer.

When my clients follow up on quotes and proposals, they find that customers love it.

They appreciate it.

And best of all: as I experienced with the contractors, *the competition isn't doing it.*

Customers value our follow-up, but we do not do it.

Much more on following up on quotes and proposals in Chapter 29.

Asking for a Referral

Have you ever stood with a group of people in a social setting, perhaps with a drink in your hand where somebody asks for a recommendation for a service provider?

Perhaps they ask for a chiropractor who can help their ailing back, without making them sign up for a multi-week plan that forces them to visit three times a week.

Or maybe they ask for a dentist who can clean their teeth without poking them and causing pain.

Or, possibly, they request a lawn service that knows not to cut the grass when it's raining.

What do other people in the group do when such a request is made? How do they react?

They almost *trip over each other,* in their haste to recommend *their* person.

"You need to use my chiropractor. He's fabulous."

"No, listen, my chiropractor is different from everybody else. He needs only one visit to fix you up."

"Wait, let me tell you about my guy. He's fabulous!"

Right?!

People are literally arguing with one another, making the case for *their* provider.

They want you to use their person.

People love giving referrals, but we do not ask for them.

Your customers are very happy with your work. Again, I know this because they've been with you for years, and they keep coming back.

Of course, they'd like to connect their friends and colleagues with a trusted, excellent provider of a product or service.

There are many reasons why people love giving referrals, which we will explore later in this book, but the big picture is that your happy customers would be more than pleased to refer you to people they know.

If only you asked.

But you rarely do.

And, in turn, they rarely do.

Much more on referrals in Chapter 32.

Why Don't We Ask?

So, if we *know* our customers would like to buy more from us . . .

If we know they're buying products and services from our competition *right now* that they could buy from us, and we would like to sell to them
. . .

If we know we should ask our customers about buying our other products and services . . .

If we know we should follow up on quotes and proposals more . . .

And if we know customers love giving referrals . . .

Why don't we ask the did you know question?

Why don't we follow up?

Why don't we ask for referrals?

Why don't we ask?

Come to think of it, why don't we ask for the business *every* time we talk to a customer? (See Chapter 26.)

And why don't we use the phone more? Most salespeople actually go out of their way to *avoid* the phone. (See Chapter 25.)

We would only benefit from making these communications.

And our customers would benefit a great deal!

So why don't we ask?

The Reason Is the Greatest Single Problem in All of Sales

We don't ask because we are afraid.

We don't ask because of fear.

Fear of what?

- Fear of rejection. What if they say "No"?
- Fear of failure. What if I won't succeed?
- Fear of upsetting the customer. What if they yell at me?
- Fear of losing the customer. What if this customer leaves me forever (because I let them know about another product I can provide)?
- Fear of shame or embarrassment. What would I tell my colleagues? What would I say to my family?

A few chapters from now, we will go through these fears, one at a time. Then we will *reject* them, one at a time.

But for now, understand that fear has cost you an awful lot of money.

And it has cost your customers some amazing opportunities to do more business with you. They've missed out on benefiting more from the wonderful value you can provide them.

Fear is the single greatest killer of sales growth, for individuals and companies alike.

And this book is about how to overcome it. *Selling Boldly* teaches you how to quickly and easily identify fear; how to develop the critical positive mindset shifts and attitudes, put forth by the incredibly valuable field of positive psychology, that will inoculate you against fear—these attitudes are the enemy of fear; and how to easily train yourself to think in a way that leaves no room for the insidiousness of fear, by immersing yourself in the glowing feedback, emotion, and experiences of your happy customers. Then we discuss the fast, simple, no-cost sales techniques that have been proven, again and again, to quickly and significantly grow sales. And finally, we talk about rolling out this powerful Selling Boldly system for yourself, personally, and also what it looks like if done systematically at your organization.

Here's a more detailed overview:

- In the first few chapters, I introduce the major problem in sales: fear. It has cost you so much money and it keeps you from doing what you *know* you should do.

- Then, Part II digs into 10 critical mindset shifts for dramatic sales growth. Are you selling proactively or reactively? Confidently or fearfully? Boldly or meekly? I lay out the differences between opposing sets of approaches, and explain why the positive one will lead you to dramatically more sales success. This part of the book is about how to *think,* because we can't outsell our thinking. If you are fearful and meek, that is how you sell. If you are confident and bold, you sell this way. The latter makes a lot more money, and in this section I will teach you how to get there.

- Part III examines *how* to obtain these positive mindsets. There is one very simple thing you can do to shift how you *think* about what you do so that you can shift to much higher sales. That very simple thing is to systematically talk to your happy (not complaining) customers, and seek to understand what they like best about working with you. If you ask them, they will tell you.

- Next, Part IV lays out more than ten simple sales-growth communications techniques for you customers and prospects. These have been carefully designed and fine-tuned over many years of implementation with my clients, and most of them take just a few seconds to put into practice. Example: *What else are you buying elsewhere that I may be able to help you with?* That's a three-second question, but it has made my clients hundreds of millions of dollars over the years! Sales growth comes from taking action, so if you'd like to jump straight to what to *do,* read this first. But then go back to read the earlier parts of this book on how to develop the appropriate mindset to execute these communications confidently, boldly, optimistically, and joyfully.

- Finally, Chapter 36 examines how salespeople *and* managers and executives can implement these systems at your firm. If you're an owner, CEO, president, GM, or head of sales, I will teach you how to install this *thinking* and *action* in your organization. For the mechanics on implementing and enjoying the benefits of Selling Boldly at your company, read this.

Throughout the book, you will find planning forms and tools to help you implement the Selling Boldly system. To create strategic, dependable sales growth, we need to infuse some proactive sales actions (the ones detailed in Part IV) into our otherwise generally reactive day. Use the tools to organize and plan your thoughts and actions and also make them a launch point for implementing our simple but powerful revenue-growing communications techniques.

2

The Massive Cost of Fear in Sales

If you sell, fear has probably cost you, personally, millions of dollars.

If you work for a company that generates $5 million in annual revenue, fear has cost your firm tens of millions of dollars over the years.

If the company is a $20 million business, fear has cost the firm *hundreds* of millions of dollars over the years. And if the company does $100 million annually, the total lost is in the billions.

But this is just individual firms. If we think about the sales lost across industries, or neighborhoods, cities, states, and nations, over years and decades, we're talking about many *trillions*.

This includes the immense amount of money salespeople have lost out on in take-home pay and in vacations not taken; the losses to the local economy not injected with this money; the investments businesses have not made, thereby hurting their suppliers; and *the customers not helped*.

I know the impact of fear on sales because I've worked with hundreds of companies and thousands of salespeople on the topic of revenue growth.

My clients add 10 to 20 percent, and often a lot more, to their sales growth annually. We accomplish this by systematically making the simple communications laid out in Part IV.

But we don't start there with my clients (nor in this book); we start with mindset. Because how you think, how you deal with fear of rejection and failure, is how you sell.

It is impossible to outsell your mindset.

If you are confident and optimistic and bold, you will enthusiastically and joyfully make the pitches to customers and prospects that growth requires. You will proactively pick up the telephone. You'll ask for referrals. You'll follow up on quotes and proposals.

But if you are fearful and cautious, you will avoid this work. You will seek refuge in less risky activities. Like email. And "research."

But let me be clear: nearly *all* salespeople deal with fear. It's human. We are wired to have it, and to avoid the situations that might make it come true.

You are not unique if you deal with fear; you are with the great majority.

Conversely, if you can consistently make the simple customer communications that lead to fast sales growth *in spite of your fear,* you will stand far above the sales crowd.

In this book, I arm you with the tools, the actions, and the thinking techniques to do this.

If you work through the tools and actions in this book—*and do the work*—you will find yourself selling much, much more, and fast.

Fear Is Automatic

The thing about fear in sales—and *all* types of fear—is that it happens automatically. We just have it. We've learned it over our entire lives. When does it start? When we are children. When our classmates reject us as friends. When we are left out of a group. When we are not one of the early picks for the kickball team. As we get older, we get rejected by potential dates. In organized sports, we can get cut while trying out for a team. Rejection can come from applying to colleges and universities, and then, of course, by companies that fire us—or don't even offer us a job.

These fears are in us.

They rear their ugly heads automatically.

But dealing with them requires (1) awareness of these fears and (2) proactive countermeasures. Anything worthwhile or good requires some effort. To begin, let's identify and define the fears specifically, and then detail what they make us do and also what they keep us from doing. At the end of this chapter, I give you a very simple two-step process to deal with your fears.

How to Leverage This with Your Customers

This dynamic holds true for everybody who reads or watches the news, including your customers.

We live in a scary world.

There is disease and disaster and war and the threat of war.

Nearly every political campaign descends into negativity. The positive campaigner is a rarity (and he or she usually loses).

The news media is happy to report all this negativity because it brings eyeballs—and the more eyeballs, the more the media is paid by advertisers.

On top of this, the customers of your customers are always complaining, rarely happy.

Altogether, on many days, your customers probably feel like they're barely able to keep their heads above the water.

What can we do?

In our own little way, we can help our customers.

With the right mindset (stay tuned for Part II!), we can be an island of calm and dependability and positivity for our customers in a storm of negativity and heartbreak.

We will do what we say we will do.

We will be reliable.

If there is an issue or problem with their order, we will communicate with them proactively. We won't wait until they call us to find out. We will tell them ourselves.

We will take care of our customers.

We will be present.

We will call them not only when we need something, but also to check in with them and say hello.

We will offer to help them with even more products and services than they are buying now. And they will be grateful.

Be an island for your customers.

Bring your customers peace. Bring them positivity.

Bring them confidence.

These are rare commodities in today's world.

It's not hard to stand out from the crowd.

The competition isn't doing these things.

Your customers will be grateful for you.

And they will come to you again and again with their business and with their trust.

What We Are Afraid Of

Let's define the fear. When we say that fear has cost you many sales and much money, here are the specific fears that nearly all salespeople deal with.

Fear of Rejection

What if they say, "No"?

   *What if they reject **me**?*

This is the big one.

All people try to avoid rejection.

There is nothing pleasant or enjoyable about it.

Nobody wants to be rejected, and of course, who can blame us for feeling this way? I feel it too, in my own sales work. Everybody feels it.

We perceive it personally. And we perceive it emotionally.

We perceive it as a rejection of *me.*

But the customer is not rejecting *us,* is she?

She is merely saying no to our product, or service, or the value she perceives those things delivering to her, as compared to what she currently has.

The customer does not reject us personally.

But that is precisely how we perceive it.

Fear of Failure

What if I don't succeed?

   Does this makes me a failure?

Here's how humans perceive failure:

Failing is final.

There is no coming back from failure.

It's a permanent blight on our careers.

This customer will never buy from us, until the end of time.

Failure is forever.

It's the opposite of success, and we don't want to be that.

But if the customers tells us *no,* have we really failed?

Have we failed with this customer? No, they simply told us they don't want *this product or service at this time.* That's all they're saying.

Have we failed at being salespeople? Of course not. We are very good at what we do. *You* are very good at what you do.

Have we failed as humans, if this customer tells us *No?*

Absolutely not. In fact, the opposite is true:

We get to move on!

Or, we get to schedule our next follow-up with this customer.

We've succeeded!

But we fear failure, and that keeps us from doing the incredibly important work of selling. Fearing failure and the rejection that can come with it is a concrete barrier between you and more money; between you and more success; between you and more happiness.

Fear of Not Being Liked

What if they hate me?

I want them to like me!

This one, like the two before it, goes back to our childhoods.

When we are young, in school, we try to fit in.

We work to win approval.

We *want* people to like us. It feels good to be liked, but pretty terrible to feel disliked by our peers.

If we call customers and check in, and ask them if they're interested in other products or services, we fear that they will dislike us—that they will be turned off to us.

You: "Listen, I know you use this other product, but you don't buy it from us. I love working with you, and I'd enjoy adding this product to the items we supply you. What do you think?"

Customer: "I hate you! You're terrible!"

Sound feasible?

Right.

It's not.

None of these fears really are.

Fear of Upsetting the Customer

What if they yell at me?

What if they talk badly about me to my boss or to others?

Just as we want the customer to *like* us, we want them to be *happy* with us.

Worse, we fear the angry customer.

Angry customers yell at us.

And if you're in the manufacturing or distribution space—or the medical device space, or technology, or services; basically, in *most* spaces—customers tend to yell a lot. In fact, if they're calling, it's highly likely they're unhappy. Because if they're pleased, there's little reason to call, and most customers do not.

So we *hate* being yelled at.

Once again, this is an innately human emotion—the fear of upsetting somebody, *especially* a customer.

That's what makes this fear—and all of the ones listed here—so damaging.

It's a totally normal reaction in the face of being asked to do what is abnormal or uncomfortable to most people: sell.

Fear of Shame or Embarrassment

What would I tell my colleagues?

How would people judge me if I lose this account?

Who wants to explain to the boss that we lost the account?

Who wants to tell others that we got rejected?

It doesn't feel good, and we don't want to present ourselves in the negative light of failure.

Who wants to tell our families that we didn't get the business?

What if they think less of us?

What do I tell my kids?

These are the fears we experience.

Of course, any colleague who sells, or manages people who sell, will know immediately that rejection is a part of this life. A big part.

And your family will know it too. It's not your first no and it won't be your last.

It's no big deal, really.

There's nothing whatsoever to be ashamed of or embarrassed about.

You asked. You followed up. You went for the yes.

So you got a no instead.

Who cares?

They're missing out on working with you on this.

It's Not Just the Fear—It's What We Imagine It Will Lead To

As though the fears detailed here are not enough, our brains create *consequences* for their coming true.

And like the fears themselves, these consequences are shaped automatically. We are not aware of their formation and we rarely really even think it through to the consequence. *We simply avoid the behaviors that cause us to feel fear!*

So, for the fears described here—fear of rejection, failure, not being liked, upsetting the customer, and being embarrassed—what are the consequences? If these fears come true, there are terrible consequences that our brains will try to avoid.

I must emphasize as strongly as possible that none of the following potential consequences are rooted in reality. None of them have a good chance (or, pretty much, *any* chance) of happening, but we experience them as *truth*. Of course, they are in our unconscious imagination—*they are not real*—but for our fearful minds, these consequences are as real as the telephone they make us avoid:

- **I'll lose the customer.** The customer will leave me forever. If I offer the product they are not buying now, they will get really angry and leave me, even though they've been with me for 15 years. If I ask for a referral from my happy customer, he will be so turned off that he will leave me even though he has been buying from our company for decades.

- **I'll go broke.** Remember, these consequences are absurd, and we process them automatically, usually without us even being aware of them—in our subconscious. If I lose this customer, it won't be long before the others leave me also, and *then* how will I make money? Before long, I won't have any money.

- **I'll lose my home.** Yep, this is the natural consequence of going broke.

- **I won't be able to provide for my family.** They depend on me, and if this customer rejects me, or gets mad at me, I won't be able to support my family.

Silly, right?

But, because these consequences live outside of our conscious awareness, *they drive our behavior.*

Our deeply-rooted fears and their imagined consequences literally affect what we do—and don't do—every hour of every day in our work.

They are in control of us.

They are in control of our money.

They are in control of our success.

But things are not as dire as they sound. It is not difficult to disarm these fears, and do the right thing *in spite of them.* It's fast and easy to shine a light on them and realize how absurd they are. But while the fears are automatic, their countermeasures require some conscious effort and attention. More on this shortly.

What Fear Makes Us Do

How do we behave when we are afraid?

What does fear do to us?

Because fear is automatic, requiring no active attention on our part, and also because our imagination creates consequences to the fear mostly subconsciously, *fear's impact on our behavior also occurs automatically.* We are not aware that our behavior is determined by fear. This requires no thought or attention from us; it's a reactive process. *Fear drives our real-world behavior in the sales profession, but we have no idea of this.*

Here are the things that fear makes us do:

- **It makes us reactive, instead of proactive.** The customer is calling with a problem or urgent issue, and we better deal with it for fear of losing the customer! And we better not ask for a referral during this call (which would require asking a five-second question), because the customer might get angry and then leave us forever.

- **It makes us email instead of call or visit.** Email is safer, and less intrusive, and the rejection is less personal. *I've sent an email; I've succeeded!* No you haven't! You've done nothing! What are the chances the customer will even *see* your email, much less reply to it?

- **It makes us procrastinate.** Fear leads pretty directly to avoiding the things that we *know* are important. It prevents action. We won't follow up on that outstanding quote because it might anger the customer. After all, they'd call *us* if they were ready to buy, right? Wrong, they're busy. They're not thinking about your quote. (We dig into this more than once in the coming pages.)

- **It makes us perfectionists.** Perfection and procrastination are highly related. Often, both characteristics are present prominently in salespeople. *I can't send it if it isn't perfect!* The thing is, it will never be perfect. You will never feel like it's all the way perfect. So you will never send it. The way to deal with this is to send the communication when it's helpful, not when it's perfect. When it's helpful, and good enough, send it. Because the distance between that point and perfection is occupied by fear! And it will always prevent you from getting to perfection.

- Fear makes us behave in counterproductive ways. It makes us undermine ourselves with damaging behavior. It makes us lesser salespeople. This hurts our customers and, of course, our families.

The Incredibly Important (and Easy) Work Fear Keeps Us from Doing

Now let's talk about all the things that fear and its imagined-in-the-real-world-but-actually-real-in-our-minds consequences blocks us from doing.

- **It keeps us from communicating with our customers.** Because we don't want to bother the customer. Or annoy them. Or take up their time. Or make them angry.

- **It keeps us from picking up the phone.** Astoundingly, outside sales-people spend an average of four hours per *week* on the telephone. Much more on this in Chapter 25.

- **It keeps us from asking for the business.** We don't ask if our customer is ready to buy because we're incredibly afraid of being rejected. And asking means they *might* reject us. So we don't ask, and never give ourselves a chance at a *yes!*

- **It keeps us from offering additional products and services to our customers.** Because, God forbid, the customer might get mad at us or leave us.

- **It keeps us from following up on quotes and proposals, and closing more of them.** Reason: see above.

- **It keeps us from asking for referrals and expanding our customer base.** Reason: see above. The tragedy here is that, as discussed in the first chapter, customers love to give us referrals.

- **It keeps us from spending more time visiting our customers.** Because we think they don't have time for us, or they don't want to see us. If you asked them, they would tell you that very few suppliers come to visit them—for the same reason: fear! —and they enjoy seeing you.

We could keep going on and on but you get the idea. If there is a proactive communication that would help you sell more, and you are *not* doing much of it, the reason is fear.

Fear keeps us from doing the work that would grow our sales.

How to Deal with Fear

Here is an incredibly simple two-step process for dealing with, and diminishing, fear in sales:

First, identify the fear precisely. What are you afraid of, exactly? Almost always it will be one of the fears listed earlier in this chapter.

Second, what will happen—exactly—if this fear comes true? So, if this customer tells you *no*, what will happen?
Death?
Will you really lose the house?
Will somebody come to the house to remove the dogs?
Will the children not have milk to drink the next day?

Of course not!

None of these ridiculous things will happen.

But unless we shine a light on the fear and what we imagine the consequences to be, *we believe the fear and its consequences will come true.*

What will really happen if you get rejected by *this* customer, on *this* order?

Nothing!

Not a damn thing will happen.

Next customer!

Remember, a customer's *no* never means no forever. It merely means not at this moment.

So move on.

And sometime soon, come back to that customer and give him another moment.

If you work through these two steps when you find yourself avoiding something you know can grow your sales, you will bring your fears out of your unconscious and into the real world.

And you will realize in seconds how ridiculous and absurd they are.

But unless we do this, the imagined fear remains in your head, where it is totally real.

We dig deeply into another, tremendously effective external method to deal with fear in Part III: the incredibly positive feedback of your happy customers. But the simple method laid out here is a powerful way to disarm fear *internally*, on your own. You don't need anybody else for this: just your own mind, tuned in and focused on this topic, for about 10 seconds.

The Customers Are Afraid, Too

We end this chapter with this: the customer is afraid, too.

You are not the only one who is dealing with fear.

By dint of being human, customers also have innate fears, and theirs are no less powerful or scary than yours.

Customers are afraid their vendors will make them look bad to their boss, or their colleagues, or worst of all, to their own customers. It has happened before. In fact, if you buy from many different vendors, it has happened many times, and will continue to happen on a regular basis.

The purchasing professional's mission in life is to not be made a fool of by vendors!

The customer is also afraid of letting their customers down. If you don't get your products there on time, or send the wrong ones, or customize them incorrectly, your customer will not be able to help *their* customers. It follows that their fears are quite similar to yours, with one nuanced caveat: your customer fears losing her customer, *because of your mistakes*.

The customer is also afraid of losing her job, because of her vendors' problems.

As you can see, anyone who sells to humans is working with customers who also have to deal with fear, even if it's a somewhat different fear than we salespeople navigate.

Hopefully, this helps you deal with *your* fear, and get on top of it.

We are all afraid.

It is our nature.

3 | The Antidote to Fear: The New Science of Positive Psychology

Here is a summary of this book in one sentence: selling more, quickly, is a function of *thinking* the right way—confidently, boldly, optimistically—and then communicating your optimism systematically to your customers and prospects. To explain why this approach is true and powerful, I need to tell you a little about a relatively new field in psychology that has changed the discipline over the past 20 years. It's called "positive psychology" and it is the study of what makes us happy, as opposed to the rest of psychology, which is the study of our depression, anxiety, and other problems.

Positive psychology examines the thinking that leads to success and happiness and joy. Positive psychology seeks to explain what gives us energy, gratitude, and optimism, and, more importantly, how to take control of our thinking to manufacture it ourselves. Meanwhile, the rest of psychology is about the biology, neurology, and the treatment of the things that make us crazy.

In simple terms, then, positive psychology focuses on the *proactive pursuit* of joy (just as strategic sales growth requires proactive communications), and personal and professional success, while much of the rest of psychology examines how we *react* to stimulus (just as most sales work is conducted reactively, in response to incoming inquiries), often driven by our internal biology. Positive psychology puts our success in our own hands and brains—we can create it, and here is how.

A lot of this might sound intuitively obvious, but researchers studying human psychology really only started to explore positive psychology a few decades ago.

A Short History of Positive Psychology (and My Very Brief Time in the Field)

The American Psychological Association was founded more than 125 years ago, and for at least 100 of those years it has been focused completely and entirely on mental illness. Its seminal publication is called the *Diagnostic and Statistical Manual of Mental Disorders*. Want to read all the possible ways people can be damaged? Read the DSM. Want to study what makes people crazy? Become a psychologist.

I know, because I was supposed to be a clinical psychologist. I majored in premed psychology in college (to this day, I've never attended a formal business class), and then changed focus to clinical psychology. I attended a five-year graduate program that awards PsyD degrees, which stands for Doctor of Psychology, and emphasizes clinical (talking, not medicine prescribing) work.

I survived only one year in this graduate school. In fact, I knew that it was not for me after about three weeks. At that point, at the age of 21 and just weeks into this new five-year program—I went straight to grad school after college (and was one of the youngest people at this grad school)—I started my first business, which was, I thought, totally unrelated to psychology.

Why didn't this cutting-edge clinical psychology graduate school work for me?

Everything revolved around mental illness.

Classes focused—in their entirety—on depression, anxiety, and more profound psychotic illnesses like schizophrenia. We talked about chronic illnesses like Alzheimer's and Parkinson's, head injuries, and memory loss, and post-traumatic stress syndrome.

Most of the other students, who were a good bit older than me, seemed enthralled with this study of what damages us. Many of them worked hard on diagnosing *themselves*. There were open discussions about which disorders applied to which students.

I worked hard at being positive, because even then, as a relative child, I knew that an optimistic outlook was one of the great keys to a good and happy life. But I found it basically impossible within the walls of this graduate school and with the people in it. The terrible weight of the daily analysis of neurosis and psychosis, combined with the prospect of dealing with it all *daily, in a room, with one client after another,* launched me out of there.

Around the same time, the great psychologist Martin Seligman—whose work I studied while attending university *and* this graduate school—was starting his world-altering work on optimism and positive psychology.

In 1967, Seligman conducted famous experiments on learned helplessness in behavioral psychology. In this work, dogs that were shocked on a regular schedule would try to escape the shocks, but dogs that received shocks *irregularly,* randomly, would simply lie down and stop trying to avoid them. This was what Seligman called *learned helplessness.*

As you can see, even the widely accepted father of positive psychology focused much of his life working on psychological illness.

In the preface to his important book *Learned Optimism,* Seligman writes that he thought he was working on pessimism in writing the book. "I was accustomed to focusing on what was wrong with individuals and then on how to fix it. Looking closely at what was already right and how to make it even better did not enter my mind."

He wrote:

"The skills of becoming happy turn out to be almost entirely different from the skills of not becoming sad, not being anxious, or not being angry. Psychology has told us a great deal about pathology, about suffering, about victims and how to acquire the skills to combat sadness and anxiety. But discovering the skills of becoming happier had been relegated to amusement parks, Hollywood, and beer commercials. Science had played no role."

(*continued*)

(continued)

And so, with the first publication of Seligman's *Learned Optimism* in 1990, the foundation for the new field of positive psychology was laid.

A Key Correlation

I want to draw a key correlation between Seligman's take on optimism and my approach to growing sales.

Most sales improvement programs—like most psychology approaches—focus on fixing what is wrong. They focus on how you're screwing it up and either stopping that or doing it less.

I think that's incorrect.

I don't think you're doing it wrong.

I think you're doing it quite right.

That is why you have so many happy customers who have been with you for years. I know because I've talked to thousands of these customers, in great detail, about what you're doing right. (See Chapter 18 for details on how to do these customer interviews.)

I think your customers love you because you're doing a lot of things right.

I think if you were screwing it up, you wouldn't have customers that have been buying from you for 10 or 20 years.

You're not doing it wrong.

You're doing it quite right. You're great at what you do.

Here is the key, then: In this book, *I simply ask you to do more of it.*

Help more customers more, in the great ways that you help them.

Tell your existing customers about what else they can buy from you, because they don't know.

Bring your amazing value to prospects who are not currently buying from you.

Help more people more.

You're not doing it wrong.

You're doing it great.

I'm asking you to do it great some more!

The Powerful Impact of Positive Psychology On Sales Growth

Here are eight reasons why I believe positive psychology and successful sales growth go hand in hand—collected from my study of Martin Seligman and other positive psychology researchers, my own personal sales experiences, as well as my work with thousands of salespeople and sales leaders.

1. Over and over, I have found that growing sales is a proactive pursuit, as opposed to a reactive one. This means we are in control of growing our sales (although a lot of established salespeople who have become hunters, and not gatherers, will disagree). More on this in Chapter 7.

2. In my own life and work, I have not only seen the principles of positive psychology drive my success, but I have also actively applied them. For example, I have had entire years in my business when *every one* of my clients told me no before they told me yes. Every one of them had rejected me before working with me and paying me. This means that if I had stopped, if I had given up, if I had not persevered, I would have been paid *zero* in these years. More on perseverance in Chapter 12.

3. Going even deeper: When you sell for a living, there are, especially at first, some really lean years. Nearly all successful salespeople have experienced this in some form. It's hard to sell when you don't know if you can pay your monthly bills. What about the mortgage? However, we must keep doing the right proactive things, the ones *we know* will lead to more sales, *even when it's difficult. Even when it's scary.* Our families deserve this from us. Our customers do also. And all those prospects, who have not yet bought from you, and are currently suffering through buying from the competition—they also deserve this from you. More on doing the right work, to generate sales ASAP even when it's difficult, is in Chapter 15.

4. Sales growth is completely within our control. *It depends on our actions, which depend on our thinking.* We sell how we think. Our mindsets and perceptions directly and immediately predict our sales.

5. That is, positive salespeople always outsell negative salespeople. Who wants to buy from a negative salesperson, anyway?

6. Furthermore, happy salespeople will always outsell unhappy ones. Right?! Happy people will pick up the phone (Chapter 25), ask

for the business (Chapter 26), offer additional products and services (Chapter 27), follow up after deliveries or completion of the work (Chapter 34), and then ask for referrals (Chapter 32). Unhappy salespeople simply take less action. This leads to a lack of sales success, which leads to further unhappiness.

7. Confident and bold salespeople will outsell meek, frightened ones. Which, of course, leads to even more confidence and boldness.

8. Finally, proactive, positive, optimistic, happy, confident, and bold salespeople do something that's immensely helpful to their sales success. It's something that very few others do. These salespeople *plan,* but also *do* (this is detailed in Chapter 16). By creating a quick, easy, and straightforward plan using the planners I introduce in this book (which are the same ones my clients use), these salespeople are not at the mercy of what's incoming. They feel *in control.* Their sales growth is strategic. They know the easy, proactive communications they must make each day to strategically grow their sales. Their growth is dependable because they own it. They control it. They plan it. And then they make it happen. They *do* the work, and work the plan.

You're Not Doing It Wrong!

One of my clients paid me a terrific compliment: the owner of a large construction manufacturer and distribution company said in a video testimonial that I am not a consultant who comes to a business to tell you what you're doing wrong—to rip up your systems and processes. Rather, I am the consultant who comes in to show you all that you are doing right, and then asks you to do more of it—help more customers more—because that is how to grow sales.

This is my work, because most salespeople, and most sales managers and executives, simply don't know the myriad things that you do wonderfully well.

Why?

Because when do customers call? When they're happy?

No, customers call when they have a problem. Or when they need something, like, yesterday. Right? Nobody calls to say, "Take nine months, get it to me whenever you're ready." That's because they're busy. If it's not urgent, they're not going to call you. They're moved to pick up the phone only when something is wrong or something is needed immediately.

Just as we are moved to complain to the manager only when the waiter or waitress has made a mistake—like not bringing us our drink for 20 minutes. But we do not call the manager over to compliment the server proactively, do we? We might *tip* a bit more, but we don't communicate our compliments. We humans aren't wired that way. (We also simply want to sit and enjoy the meal with our families, just as our customers simply want to get to their work when they're busy.)

You spend your days dealing with problems and urgent matters with your customers. You must deal with this because you are in the customer service business. You must serve the customer. The problem is, as soon as you're done dealing with one problem, the next one comes in. Then the next. And the next. And you blink, and it's 4:30 P.M. and time to go home. You come back the next day and do it all over again. This is the reactive day of the typical salesperson.

Because this is how we spend our days, we begin to believe that our customers are not very happy. We begin to believe our customers are angry with us, because the people we talk to are often unhappy and maybe even yelling. We start to think that our product or service isn't very good, and we're not very good at our jobs.

And we become meeker.

We lose confidence.

We are not bold. We are the opposite: we are afraid.

But here's the thing: these customers you're talking to comprise only about 10 percent of all of your customers! The other 90 percent are perfectly happy. It's just that they're not calling you to tell you about it, because of the dynamic described earlier.

You're better than you think.

The great majority of your customers are damn happy with you.

You save them time.

You are reliable.

You return their calls quickly.

You help them look good to *their* customers, internal or external.

You have a wonderful relationship.

They feel like you are friends.

Some of your customers will say it's like you're family.

But they won't call you to tell you this.

You have to *ask them what they are happy about*. Ask them, and they will be thrilled to tell you. But we don't ask, because we are afraid.

This book teaches you how to ask your customers about what you are doing well (see Chapter 18).

You can hear from them—in their words—about how excellent you are at your work.

This book teaches you how to bust out of the fearful vicious circle of reactive problem solving for customers and enter into the righteous, virtuous circle of proactively helping more customers more, who will, in turn, be happy to thank you with their money (detailed in the next chapter).

4

The Selling Boldly System: Step 1— Get Your Mindset Right; Step 2— Behave Accordingly (Communicate Boldly)

The Selling Boldly approach to sales growth is a proven, fast, and very simple way to grow sales, based on a simple truth.

The shortest path to selling more is to communicate more with customers and prospects.

That's it.

The more that customers and prospects hear from us, the more they buy from us. The less they hear from us, the less they buy.

And that's my goal here: by the time you finish reading this book, I hope you will begin to communicate much more with people who can buy from you.

The communications I show you in Part IV are not complicated and they do not require a lot of time.

Many of them are simply questions that you drop in to existing conversations. And many of the questions take all of two seconds to ask.

Here's the thing, though: before we talk about technique, we need to discuss mindset, because, as I've already argued, you cannot outsell your thinking. If you're fearful, you sell that way. If you're confident, you sell much better. If you're thinking meekly, or cynically, your sales suffer much more than if you are thinking boldly and gratefully.

In the next part of this book, we're going to talk about these mindsets, and how they affect your success. What follows are the mindsets we will focus on. The Selling Boldly mindset—which is the healthy, powerful, ideal one for communicating more with your customers and prospects—is in the left column. On the right is the mindset that prevents most salespeople from helping their customers more, selling them more products and services, and taking home more money to their families.

Selling Boldly	Selling Fearfully
Proactive	Reactive
Confident	Fearful
Boldness	Meekness
Optimistic	Pessimistic
Grateful	Cynical
Consistent Perseverance	Quick Surrenders
Focus on Value & Relationship	Focus on Products & Services
Take Constant Communication Action	Overplan and Underexecute
Make It Look Easy	Laboring, and It Shows
Plan–Driven	Inquiry–Driven

In Part III, we discuss *how to move from the damaging mindset to the ideal one for selling more*. It is as simple as listening to your happy customers talk about what they enjoy and appreciate about working with you. It's critical to obtain this input because we spend our days dealing with customers who are either happy or need something urgently.

Then we'll detail the techniques with scripts and examples in Part IV.

And finally, I lay out the Selling Boldly process from an executive leader's perspective, and discuss how to implement this work at your organization. This is what I do every day in my consulting work with clients—implement *this* system to make sure that customer-facing people are communicating exponentially more with customers and prospects.

The Defining Characteristics of Selling Boldly

- **First and foremost, it's simple.** None of these techniques are difficult to *do*.

- **Second, the work requires very little time.** If you can give me five minutes per day, I'll show you how to make *dozens* of our sales-growth communications to customers and prospects every week. Dozens, because most of the communications require five seconds or less, in the midst of conversations you are already having.

- **Third, it costs no money to do this work.** It requires no financial investment. I will never tell you that you need to advertise more. Or that you need to carry new products. No, my experience with clients has shown that the product range you sell today, right now, can double your sales.

- **However, confidence, boldness, optimism, and gratitude—as well as the other characteristics on the left side of the table detailed earlier in this chapter—*are* required.** We need to *think* this way, so that we can consistently make the communications that sales growth demands.

- **In the Selling Boldly approach to growing sales, quantity trumps quality.** That is, the more communications we make, the more people will buy from us. And unlike products and services, communications do not need to be perfect. They merely need to be helpful.

- **These communications are snowflakes that turn into blizzards.** On their own, they are lightning fast and easy questions and messages that require five seconds or less. But do five a day (for a whopping 25 seconds!), and you have 20 per week, 100 per month, and 1,200 per year. If these communications are all did you know questions, we know that 20 percent of all did you know questions result in a new line item, where the customers buy a product or service they were not previously buying. This means you've added 240 line items. If your line items average $1,000, you've just added a quarter million dollars in sales. But if they average $5,000, you've added $1.2 million. And that's just one of the techniques. Snowflakes into blizzards.

- **The Selling Boldly system infuses some proactive actions into your normally reactive days.** It's about you taking control of your sales, and, simply, helping more customers more.

- **As such, Selling Boldly is centered around quickly planning your communications and recording their results.** One of the key pillars of this work is to quickly plan it, but then also to *do* it! Many times, we plan and plan but never do. Usually, because of fear (there's that word again!), or perfection. With this approach to growing sales, first we disarm the fear, then we eliminate the need to be perfect, then we make a plan, and most gloriously, we execute the plan! Because somebody is awaiting the results.

- **Which brings us to this: there must be accountability.** Toward the end of the book, I ask you who will hold you accountable? "Myself" is not an option. It needs to be a different human. Somebody who is able to say, "You said you would do this. How did it go?" If it's your supervisor or manager, that's perfect. But you're the boss. Who will hold *you* accountable? This doesn't work with accountability.

- **Selling Boldly brings quick wins.** For a new habit to stick, we need fast success. It can't take a year to see results. No, if you implement the approaches I lay out in this book, you will see success during *your first week of doing this*. That's how effective this is. The wins come fast because the customers love you and they're thrilled to have the opportunity to buy more from you.

You Already Know What to Do

I am not going to teach you much in this book that you don't already know.

Glad you're reading?!

Keep going, I'll explain.

You're a professional salesperson. You do this for a living. You *know*, for example, that testimonials and referrals are among the best ways we have to grow sales, right? But do you *ask* for them enough? Most people don't.

You know that calling a customer on the phone is more effective than emailing her, but you still often revert to email. Even though a call would be more effective.

You know your customers buy other products and services that you can help them with, but you don't ask them about these products. You'd like to help them, and they would like more of your help—that is why they've been with you for 5 or 10 or 20 years—but nevertheless, you don't ask them.

There is a difference between knowing what to do, and actually doing it.

I know you know.

But because you're extremely busy serving your customers, and reacting to what they need from you (and you must do this, because you are in the customer service business, even though you're in sales), you frequently don't *do* what you *know*.

A lot of life is like this. If we all did what we knew, we'd all be in great physical shape, have huge savings accounts, and never lose our temper (after all, we *know* we shouldn't!).

In sales, there are various reasons why we don't do what we know we should. Rather, there are numerous small reasons and one big one that dominates them all in regard to its impact on you, your work, and your earnings.

The small reasons are:

- You're busy. You don't have time.
- You don't think to do these things. It simply doesn't occur to you. This is fair enough.
- You don't know how. You know you should ask for referrals, but nobody has ever given you language and approaches for doing so.

And here is the big one:

We Know This Works

I am not a professional author, although I've written four books.

I also don't consider myself a professional speaker, even though I present in front of audiences just about every week.

Rather, I make my living running a consulting practice. I apply the concepts in this book to clients, like you, every day. I also happen to grow my own business with these tools.

My clients experience an average of 10 to 20 percent growth annually while applying the same concepts and approaches that are laid out in this book. I don't just write and speak about these approaches; I apply them, to clients and to my own business.

This means we *know* this works. The mindsets and actions in this book are *proven* to grow sales. Over nearly a decade, I've taught these approaches to thinking and selling to thousands of salespeople. Over the years, I've tested, edited, simplified, measured, simplified, systematized, and simplified again everything in this book. The reason these approaches are simple is because if it even *smells* of complexity, salespeople won't be interested in it. Because you're busy. You're responding to customer issues and concerns all day. It's not like you're sitting around with free time. You're slammed. And you're in the business of serving your customers, even if they're demanding, and *especially* when they call complaining. So it better be simple. And it better be fast. And it better be free. Because if it were complicated, or difficult, or cost money, you would—rightfully—simply not do it.

So, the approaches presented here are *proven* to work.

We don't *hope* this works.

We don't *wish* this works.

We *know* this works, because company after company, and salesperson after salesperson, enjoys sustained dramatic sales growth when applying the thinking and selling approaches presented here.

And, so, if we know this works, the question is: *Will you do it?*

I'll tell you exactly what to do.

But your sales will grow only if you *do* some of what you read about.

In this book, I tell you what to do.

The question is, will you do it?

Will you do the work?

Will you *apply* what you learn?

That's the key to everything.

Reading will make you smarter.

But doing will make you money.

What will you *do?*

There Are No Secrets

There are no magic bullets for sales.

There are no secrets.

And as I've said before, there's probably nothing here that you don't already know.

People love easy ways out. I know I do.

I love the quick and easy sale.

But as we know, this is not the rule. It is the great exception.

Most sales require our effort and our focus, over an extended period of time.

The sale is the reward for the work.

If you wait to execute only the easy sales, refusing to put in the work that most sales require, you will probably find yourself short on money.

There are no short cuts in our business.

There is only the work.

We must do the work.

We must communicate.

We must show our customers we care.

There are no secrets.

There is only the grind.

You know the sales grind, right?

The repetitive actions that sales require.

The grind involves, for example, telling our customers over and over the various things that they can buy from us.

Even though we've told them many times, they don't remember.

That's why they tell this awful statement that every salesperson has heard many times in their careers: "I didn't know you did that!"

They don't know, even though we told them.

They don't remember.

Because they're busy.

They have their own fires. They have their own problems.

So they forget.

Which is why we must grind.

We must communicate. Always. But always with value. We must always communicate helpfully.

We must help our customers.

We must do the work.

We owe them this, and we owe our families this.

There are no secrets, and no magic bullets.

There is only the work.

Will you do the work?

5

The *Selling Boldly* Toolkit: Planners and Downloads

There are really only three ways to grow sales organically:

1. Sell to more or different customers.
2. Sell more or different products to existing customers.
3. Communicate more or differently about your products and services to customers and prospects.

The planners in this chapter comprise the Selling Boldly Toolkit and they are designed to help you systematically and proactively pursue all three of these approaches. The planners ask you to think of and write down *people* (customers and prospects); *what you can sell them* (products or services) to help them a great deal; and *how you will communicate with them*.

**Download the Selling Boldly Toolkit at www.goldfayn
.com.**

There is no cost.
Because I want you to take control of your sales.
I want you to be confident.
I want you to be bold.
I want you to help your customers and prospects more.
They deserve that from you.
And you deserve the additional business they bring you.

The sales planners are simple worksheets designed to help you quickly plan your proactive sales work and take control of your sales. They will help you infuse proactive actions into your otherwise reactive day. They will help you feel in control of your work, to *take* control of your sales work, and to communicate with your customers and prospects.

Guidelines for Using the Selling Boldly Sales Planners

Before I introduce the planners, some quick guidelines.

I want you to fill them out quickly, and spend most of your time taking action.

With some practice, you'll be able to complete *all* of the monthly planners in 30 minutes or so, with 10 to 15 minutes on "The One-Page Sales Planner," which lays out your week of proactive action.

I want you to plan, but also do.

Too many people plan, plan again, plan some more, and then don't do anything on their plan.

It's why there is an entire cottage industry around testing, evaluating, and discussing task-planning software on the Internet.

When it comes to planning, we humans spend far more time making them than doing them.

To grow sales, the key is to make *quick* plans, and execute them daily.

Here, then, are the planners we'll use throughout this book to sell boldly, and sell more.

It Begins with This Mindset Planner

SELLING BOLDLY	Applying the New Science of Positive Psychology to Dramatically Increase Your Confidence, Happiness, and Sales

THE SELLING BOLDLY MINDSET PLANNER

Date Range:

Three Recent Sales Wins I'm Proud Of
1.
2.
3.

**Three Specific Things I'm Grateful For
(Personal or Professional)**
1.
2.
3.

**Top Three Things My Customers Value and Appreciate
About Working With Me**
1.
2.
3.

**Three People (Or Groups of People) Who Deserve
For Me To Take Action This Week, Even When It's Difficult**
1.
2.
3.

**Top Three Perseverance Priorities
(I Will Try Again Here This Week)**
1.
2.
3.

ALEX • GOLDFAYN

Get digital versions of this and other planners at www.goldfayn.com/Copyright 2018 Alex Goldfayn

I'd like you to fill out the "The Selling Boldly Mindset Planner" weekly, and keep it in front of you.

It's designed to help you get into the right state of mind—that is, proactive, confident, bold, optimistic, and grateful—so that you can implement the simple communications actions we cover in Part IV.

The positive psychology experts, especially Martin Seligman, teach us that thinking through and writing down where we have succeeded and what we are grateful for, and in this case, what our customers appreciate about us and where in our work we will apply perseverance, will help us be more successful.

So, use this planner on a weekly basis.

I review this planner in detail in Chapter 6.

Prepare and Use These Planners Every Two to Four Weeks

The next group of planners are designed to be written up every two to four weeks.

Or, essentially, as often as you need to.

The first is the "Proactive Call Planner."

The proactive call planner is designed to help you think about and write down *people to call*.

I want you to think about customers *and* prospects, because we rarely communicate with prospects (they don't call us, and we usually don't call them).

I review this "Proactive Call Planner" in Chapter 24.

PROACTIVE CALL PLANNER

Date Range:

What To Say On These Calls
- Just checking in.
- I was just thinking about you.
- How have you been?
- How's your family?
- What are you working on that I can help with?

Top Customers Who Can Buy More (And WHAT To Offer Them)	Customers I Haven't Talked To In Six Months Or More	Customers Who Used To Buy, But Stopped	Good Customers Who Just Received An Order (Follow-up)

Prospects I Once Talked To (3+ Months) But They Never Bought	Prospects I Know Are Buying Elsewhere Now	Prospects I've Never Talked To, But Want To Make Contact With	Prospects I'm Actively Speaking With, But Have Not Yet Bought

SELLING BOLDLY	Applying the New Science of Positive Psychology to Dramatically Increase Your Confidence, Happiness, and Sales

THE DYK PLANNER

DYK Complete List	DYK If/Then		DYK Top 7
	If The Customer Buys: DYKs:	If The Customer Buys: DYKs:	1.
			2.
			3.
	If The Customer Buys: DYKs:	If The Customer Buys: DYKs:	4.
			5.
			6.
			7.

ALEX • GOLDFAYN

Get digital versions of this and other planners at www.goldfayn.com/Copyright 2018 Alex Goldfayn

This is "The DYK Planner"—the did you know planner.

I created this to help you think about what your customers buy now, and what they *could* buy from you that they are not currently buying. There's an awful lot of money going to your competition right now that could—and should—be going to you. Use this planner to lay out how you'll sell more to those customers.

I review this planner in Chapter 27.

Plan your referral requests and results with the Selling Boldly "Referral Planner."

On the top part, I want you to think of internal referrals you can ask for—to other buyers within the same company—and also external referrals, to other companies. Then, track your progress and referrals on the bottom portion.

REFERRAL PLANNER

Date Range:

How To Ask For Referrals

➤ Who do you know, like yourself, who would benefit from working with me the way that you do?
➤ Would you like to connect us, or should I reach out and use your name?
➤ I know you're busy; so that I don't jump the gun, when do you think you might get to that?
➤ Excellent; so if I don't hear from you by then, I'll check in. Does that sound okay?

Who To Ask For INTERNAL Referrals	Who To Ask For EXTERNAL Referrals

Referral Results			
Referral From	Who	How	When

ALEX • GOLDFAYN
Get digital versions of this and other planners at www.goldfayn.com/Copyright 2018 Alex Goldfayn

We'll dive into this "Referral Planner" in Chapter 32.

Prepare and Use Your "The One-Page Sales Planner" Weekly

This planner is double-sided. The front, schedule side lays out your week, and asks you to plan which of our communications actions you will implement this week. Track your results, including the potential dollar value of your actions. The back, planning side allows you to transfer the people and companies you laid out on your longer-term planners onto your weekly planner. The planning side of the "The One-Page Sales Planner" incorporates nearly every one of the communications actions laid out in Part IV.

SELLING BOLDLY   Applying the New Science of Positive Psychology to Dramatically Increase Your Confidence, Happiness, and Sales

THE ONE-PAGE SALES PLANNER

➤ This week, I will help more people more.
➤ My customers deserve more of my great value!

Name:

Date Range:

Code	Action
Call	Proactive Call
PTS	Pivot to the Sale (Ask for the Business)
DYK	Did You Know Question
rDYK	Reserve Did You Know Question
QF/U	Quote or Proposal Follow-Up
% Biz	% of Business Question
Ref	Ask for a Referral
Comm T	Communicate a Testimonial Proactively
HWN	Hand-Written Note
PDC	Post Delivery Call

This Week's Pivots To The Sale

Day	Proactivity Tally	Actions	Results Action, Customer, Outcome	Revenue Estimated/Est. Annual/ Quoted/Sold
Monday				
Tuesday				
Wednesday				
Thursday				
Friday				

"Whether you think you can, or you think you can't, you're right!" - Henry Ford

ALEX • GOLDFAYN Get digital versions of this and other planners at www.goldfayn.com/Copyright 2018 Alex Goldfayn

SELLING BOLDLY		Applying the New Science of Positive Psychology to Dramatically Increase Your Confidence, Happiness, and Sales

Proactive Call List		This Week's DYKs		This Week's Quote Follow Ups	This Week's Referral Requests	
Name & Company	C or P	Name & Company	Product/ Service	Name & Company	Name & Company	In/Ex

This Week's Hand-Written Notes
Name & Company

This Week's Top Revenue-Potential PROSPECTS	This Week's rDYKs	This Week's Testimonial Communications	
Name & Company	Name & Company	To Name & Company	Whose Testimonial

This Week's Post-Delivery Calls
Name & Company

This Week's Top Revenue-Potential CUSTOMERS
Name & Company

Get digital versions of this and other planners at www.goldfayn.com/Copyright 2018 Alex Goldfayn

We review the "The One-Page Sales Planner" and how to use it in Chapter 35.

Ready? FIRE!!!! Aim.

That's our process to sell more.

Ready means make your bigger plans for the month in 20 to 30 minutes, and then make your weekly plan in 15 minutes or less.

FIRE means now take action daily. Live in your plan. Keep it on your desk. Keep it visible on a screen. Track your results. Example: Tuesday you planned to ask for a referral. Did you do it? How did it go? Did you get one? It's okay to not get one, but it's not okay not to ask. Swing the bat. Track your results. If you did not ask, but planned to ask, move it to tomorrow. Things come up. You won't do everything every day, but do everything you planned for the week in that week.

Aim means assess what's working and make changes going forward. If some of these actions aren't working, edit them. Change the language. Change the approach. But if they are still not working, get them out. And double down on the ones that are providing results for you.

But do not get stuck aiming. And aiming. And aiming.

We must fire.

Because the gunpowder *will* go bad.

(How many times have you made a long list on one of those task management programs, did a little of it, and then came back to it three months later to find it had lost all relevance. Yet you spent valuable time on it, getting it just right. That's what happens with bad gunpowder—use it immediately or it becomes useless.)

The 10 Critical Mindset Shifts for Dramatic Sales Growth

Selling Boldly	Selling Fearfully
Proactive	Reactive
Confident	Fearful
Boldness	Meekness
Optimistic	Pessimistic
Grateful	Cynical
Consistent Perseverance	Quick Surrenders
Focus on Value & Relationship	Focus on Products & Services
Take Constant Communication Action	Overplan and Underexecute
Make It Look Easy	Laboring, and It Shows
Plan-Driven	Inquiry-Driven

6

About These Critical Thinking Shifts

The 10 mindset shifts laid out in this section have to do with how we view and approach our work.

Many of these 10 mindsets are core components of the approaches espoused by positive psychology. In this part of the book, we apply these concepts to the selling profession, and to you, the sales professional.

Each one will detail the *ideal* mindset, and its opposite, which is the one most of us struggle with.

The goal is to move toward the ideal position.

Good news! Even though I'm detailing 10 key thinking changes to sell more quickly, there is one way to attain *all* of these ideal mindsets: talk to your happy customers and listen to their glowing feedback. That simple action will lead you to shift to the ideal mindset in each of the examples listed in this section of the book. I'll dive deeply into how to develop this in Part III.

Which means making the shift is not complicated.

But it's incredibly valuable to your success, your company's growth, and the income you take home to your family.

These Mindsets Snowball, Building on Each Other

A fascinating thing about the mindsets in the table at the start of the chapter is that the positive ones build on one another and the negative ones do too. They spiral, or snowball, one onto the next.

For example, on the right side of the table: if you are fearful, you behave meekly and your work is reactive. You are pessimistic and increasingly cynical, and you have difficulty persevering, making you less likely to follow up. In your sales work, you focus on products and services, rather than your relationships, and because of these things you tend to avoid taking necessary action. Because you are not certain in yourself or your great value, and you don't want to bother or annoy the customers, you won't communicate with them as much as you should. They won't hear from you much because you feel fearful and behave meekly. You work hard, and your hard work shows, because you spend your days responding to a mountain of incoming inquiries. As a consequence, you find it extremely difficult to find the time to proactively communicate with your customers and prospects. There, we've covered the entire right side of the table!

Now, let's do the same for the left side—the good and righteous side: if you know and believe in the tremendous value you provide to your customers, you are confident in your thinking, and bold in your behavior. You infuse some proactive sales work into your otherwise reactive day. You are optimistic about the outcome before you call or visit your customer. You also move through your day gratefully, appreciating your opportunities, customers, and yes, even the struggles and challenges (because you get to work on resolving them!). You persevere as a matter of course, understanding that *no* almost never means *no forever*. You focus on your value and your relationships rather than your products and services, and you're constantly taking action, instead of thinking about it. On top of all that, you make it all look easy, even though it requires some hard work. You are plan-driven, laying out your proactive communications quickly at the start of each week, to make sure you don't spend *all* of your time bouncing around from one incoming customer problem to the next.

See how it works?

Now let's play out a scenario: you've had a bad morning. Dealing with the kids on your way out the door was frustrating, and you're feeling grouchy on your drive in. You get to the office and a customer calls with a complaint, then another customer, and another. By 10 A.M., you're feeling annoyed. *At this point you don't feel grateful for these customers. For their ability to buy more. For their trust. For their belief in you.* You feel intruded upon (you're human). You think about them—and this is rare for you—with some cynicism. Well, once you allow yourself to be cynical, pessimism creeps in next, doesn't it? *Here comes another complaint!* With this mindset, it's difficult to behave boldly, and think confidently, so we start trending toward meeker execution. Fear marches in: *Why are they all so angry today?* Will you be able to persevere and try again with this outlook? Probably not effectively. This day is probably lost. You're in too deep.

This means you must bounce back quickly. Tomorrow must be better. We can't let these days build up. We must go to our customer testimonials and marinate our minds in the incredibly positive feedback from our happy customers (as detailed in Part III). We must remind ourselves how good we are. *How lucky am I? This is how I help people. Look how happy they are. Today, I will work to help more people like this.* And now you've departed the dark side, the right side of the table. You're in the light. You're on the Selling Boldly side. You're confident, bold, optimistic, proactive, and grateful. You're helping people again, and today, you're making lots of money!

That's how these mindsets work.

You Have a Choice

Here's the thing about all of the critical sales mindset shifts that follow: we get to decide!

It's magical!

We can *choose* to approach the world confidently or fearfully.

It's up to us.

We can decide if we will spend a minute or two thinking about what we are grateful for today, or if we will go through our days cynically.

We can decide if we will try to take some proactive actions today, or if we will spend the *entire* day reactively. Even though it may not feel that way now, it's completely up to us!

We're in control of how we view the world.

And these mindsets are worldviews for salespeople.

We can decide that it's going to be a good day.

Or a bad day.

Either way, we're right.

You can choose, *right now,* as you sit and read this book, that you're going to look for techniques that you can implement in your sales work. You can review the approaches that are right for you, choose the ones you think will work well, try them, and then assess them for success.

Or, you can decide right now that this is not for you. You know how to sell. You're good. Your customers are good. They don't need anything more from you.

And you will be right either way.

That's the magic of being us.

We get to decide.

So if we're doing the job anyway—whether it's getting up in the morning, or going to work, or reading this book, or trying to support our family, or trying to support our organization's goals—why not make the right choice?

You have to *do* it anyway.

Why not choose the mindset that will make you money?

You get to choose.

Make the right choice!

"The Selling Boldly Mindset Planner"

SELLING BOLDLY	Applying the New Science of Positive Psychology to Dramatically Increase Your Confidence, Happiness, and Sales

▨ THE SELLING BOLDLY MINDSET PLANNER

Date Range:

Three Recent Sales Wins I'm Proud Of
1.
2.
3.

Three Specific Things I'm Grateful For (Personal or Professional)
1.
2.
3.

Top Three Things My Customers Value and Appreciate About Working With Me
1.
2.
3.

Three People (Or Groups of People) Who Deserve For Me To Take Action This Week, Even When It's Difficult
1.
2.
3.

Top Three Perseverance Priorities (I Will Try Again Here This Week)
1.
2.
3.

ALEX • GOLDFAYN
Get digital versions of this and other planners at www.goldfayn.com/Copyright 2018 Alex Goldfayn

Go to www.Goldfayn.com and download a copy of "The Selling Boldly Mindset Planner."

I'd like you to spend 5 to 10 minutes filling it out, once a week, preferably before your week begins.

1. Write out three recent sales wins you are proud of.

2. Detail three specific things you are grateful for.

3. List three things your customers value and appreciate about working with you. No wrong answers.

4. Write down the names of three people or groups of people who deserve to have you sell more. Think family, colleagues, customers, prospects, owners, and so on.

5. Name three areas you will persevere with this week. A specific customer, perhaps, or a deal you've been working on. Where will you try again?

Once you write it, look at it every day.

Keep it on top of your desk.

I want you to see this positivity.

I want you to marinate in this positivity.

Because you're a lot better than you think.

I want you to have this positivity in your conscious mind daily.

If you do, you will find the selling work detailed here quite comfortable and easy.

And you'll make more money in a hurry.

Selling Boldly	Selling Fearfully
Proactive	Reactive
Confident	Fearful
Boldness	Meekness
Optimistic	Pessimistic
Grateful	Cynical
Consistent Perseverance	Quick Surrenders
Focus on Value and Relationship	Focus on Products and Services
Take Constant Communication Action	Overplan and Underexecute
Make It Look Easy	Laboring, and It Shows
Plan-Driven	Inquiry-Driven

7 | Proactive Selling versus Reactive Selling

As discussed in Chapter 2, most salespeople spend their days reactively.

Customers call when they need something, or when they have a problem.

We must serve the customer. There is no choice. We must address their concerns.

We do. And then, almost immediately, the next customer's concern or urgent need arrives. Right?

And this is how we salespeople live, Monday through Friday. Reactively.

The problem is, sales growth requires proactive work.

We cannot react our way to strategic growth.

We *can* react our way to accidental, random growth.

But we become a pinball, bouncing around from one incoming concern to the next.

If the right inquiries or problems come in, we *might* grow. If we're lucky. But it's not up to us. Of course, if the wrong concerns come in, we must react to those also. And in this case, we do not grow.

When we react our way to growth, it is not in our control.

We cannot predict it.

We cannot plan for it.

We cannot expect it.

We are left to simply wonder if this year we will be lucky and possibly grow.

But we might not.

Because we are not in control.

Random inquiries are in control.

This chapter examines two additional ways of considering reactive selling versus proactive selling. One of them is from a medical professor at the Mayo Clinic. The other is from a sales growth consultant in the Chicago area, me.

Default Brain versus Focused Brain

Amit Sood is a professor of medicine at the Mayo Clinic College of Medicine, and he has developed a wonderful concept for thinking and behavior. He calls it *default brain* versus *focused brain*.

Default brain is the one that's usually active and engaged.

Default brain oversees the things we do automatically, without too much thought or intention.

Default brain drives the things we do habitually, whether good or bad.

What do you do first thing in the morning?

Do you go exercise?

Or do you eat boxed cereal and other processed, sugary foods?

Whatever you do automatically or daily tends to be ruled by your default brain.

Focused brain is the opposite. It's in charge of our intentional behaviors. Focused brain controls activities that simply wouldn't happen unless we plan and execute them with purpose.

When you try new things, or try to build new habits like the activities we're talking about in this book, you engage your focused brain.

Quick quiz:

Responding to incoming phone calls and addressing the problems or urgent needs of our customers is a default brain or focused brain activity?

Making a phone call to a longtime customer to see if he can benefit from another product or service you can provide that they do not currently buy . . . . Is this engaging the default brain or focused brain?

Answers: Reacting to what's incoming is a default brain activity. Meanwhile, intentionally communicating with and educating customers and prospects is a focused brain activity.

Predictable sales growth requires the focused brain.

Are You Hunting or Gathering?

In the olden days, as my eight-year-old son Noah says, before grocery stores, when humans lived in the wilderness, some people hunted and others gathered.

Hunters went to find meat for their community. Usually, it was not nearby. It needed to be found, and then captured, or converted. The hunters went to where the food was and brought it back to their families.

Others in the community gathered food. They looked around them, examined what was immediately nearby (usually growing), and collected what was there.

There is a similar structure in sales, but the hunters are few and far between. In sales, a hunter goes to find the business, and brings it back to the company. They seek it, they nurture it, they build trust, develop relationships, learn about their prospects, offer great value (even before the prospect becomes a customer), and earn the business. Hunters go find sales.

Salespeople who gather, conversely, collect what comes in. They answer the phone, and fill the orders. They serve the customer. They must do this, of course. We're all in the customer service business. And if the customer has a need, or a concern, we must address it. But if we do nothing else—and most of us do not—gatherers are at the complete mercy of what's incoming.

The Silent Transition from Hunting to Gathering

About two to three years into a sales career, an imperceptible shift occurs for many salespeople. It happens gradually, not suddenly, and quietly, without fanfare. Most of the time, even the salesperson doesn't know it's happening. This is what it looks like:

When the salesperson begins the job, there is no book of business. And there are no sales and little money.

Worse, there's nothing to gather. We've planted no seeds, because we haven't been on the job long enough.

And because we need to eat, or make sure our family eats, we hunt.

We build prospect lists.

We use the phone. Calling people who we might be able to help.

We go visit prospects.

We ask for referrals.

We ask for the business.

We follow up on our quotes and proposals. Because we need the business. We need to eat.

And this is how we build up our sales.

With all of this positive, proactive work, people begin to buy.

And because we serve them well, they come back. And they keep buying.

We get busier.

More customers buy, and buy again.

Then, something begins to happen.

These customers start to call not just with orders, but also when something is wrong.

The phone starts to ring more. You have less and less free time.

You are serving the customer.

Meanwhile, your previous proactive efforts continue to bring in some new customers, because it was good, righteous work you did when you were hunting.

But these incoming new customers start to trail off, because you are not keeping up with the proactive outreach.

More and more you deal with urgent requests or problems.

You become an experienced sales person.

You become busier and busier.

The phone now rings all day.

A good thing, right?

This is what you have worked for.

Well, theoretically, it's great when the phone rings.

But this makes us reactive.

It leaves little time for the proactive hunting work that makes your sales so successful.

And thus, the transition is complete.

You have become a gatherer.

You have become reactive.

Because your success is no longer within your control—that is, serving the customer extremely well *does not* necessarily lead to more work from that customer—you are no longer in control of your success.

Worse, you have become fearful.

You fear rejection and failure.

You avoid the work that puts you in the position to be rejected, which happens to be the work of hunting.

You are a gatherer.

And nobody even noticed it happen.

And when you become a gatherer, you tend to remain one. Months pass first, then years, and then the decades. The time flies, because the phone calls keep coming, and you must react to them. Twenty or 30 years later, you look back, and you realize you've spent much of your career living on sales that were first made—or developed from—those early hunting days. Even many of the new sales can be traced back to those early ones.

Imagine—just imagine!—if you had injected some hunting into those ensuing years.

What if, in the midst of all the gathering, you went on a hunt or two every once in a while?

They don't have to be week-long hunts or even day-long hunts.

They can be one-minute hunts, done daily.

Hunting can be telling a long-time customer what else they can buy from you.

Or asking for referrals.

Or regularly asking for the business.

Each one of the preceding is a five-second action.

Do a total of 10 of these proactive hunting actions, and you're at a whopping 50 seconds.

Fifty seconds of hunting. Every day.

That's what this book is about.

We will implement the proactive actions that sales growth demands.

Busting Out of the Vicious, Reactive Selling Circle

The more we work reactively, the more we work reactively. It's a vicious circle, feeding on itself, sucking up your time, crushing creativity, and making plans and to-do lists basically obsolete. Because, who has the time?

Here's what the reactive vicious circle looks like.

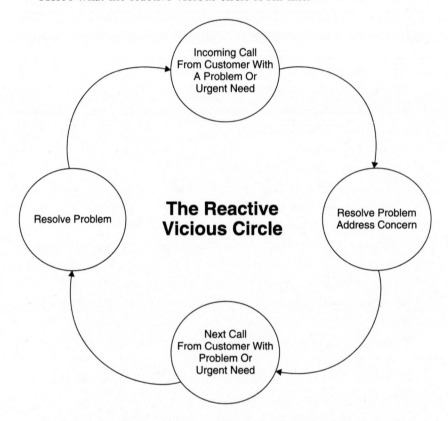

You come into work, and the phone rings. A customer has a problem. You solve it. Your default brain is at work. You put down the phone. Then . . . the phone rings again. Who's on the phone now? A customer wants to order something that he needs ASAP. Immediately. If he's calling, it's urgent. So we handle it. Put down the phone, and it rings again. We do this again and again, until it's time to go home. The next morning, we come in and do it again. The next week, we do it again. Next month? Again. Call after call, year after year, problem after urgent need after immediate concern. Entire careers pass through the decades this way.

Their phone calls to us are reactive! That is, our customers are doing reactive work when they call us. Their own customer, internal or external, or their boss, is telling them to get it now. Now! So they call, stressed and breathless, and transfer all that to you. They place *their* fire on your desk. And you must put it out. Because that's what we do. That's our job: help the customer. We service the customer.

The problem is, of course, our sales, and the money we take home, are totally dependent upon the inquiries that come in. If the right concerns come in, we might grow. If not, we won't. We are not in control. Randomness is in control, and that's no way to live, especially for salespeople.

As a result, we need to bust out of the reactive vicious circle, and work our way to the proactive virtuous circle.

Here's what the proactive righteous circle looks like.

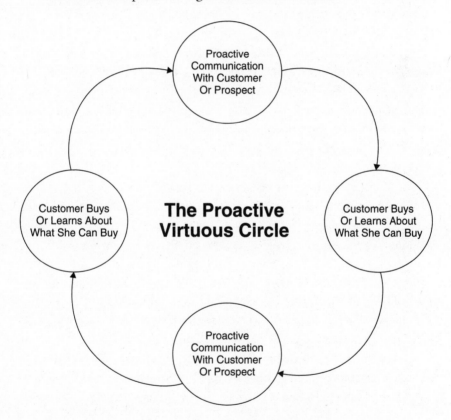

The more we work proactively, the more we work proactively.

The more we tell customers what else they can buy, the more they buy other products and services. Which leads to us getting paid more, which leads to us alerting even more customers about what else they can buy. Our focused brains are working.

The more we follow up on quotes and proposals, they more they close, and the more we are motivated to follow up on additional quotes.

The more we call our customers on the phone and experience how pleased they are to hear from us, and then watch them buy more from us, the more interested we become in calling other customers.

Reactive Selling versus Proactive Selling

Proactive work generates sales you would not otherwise have.

Reactive work tends to simply put out fires.

Proactive work takes control of your sales growth. *You* are in charge. Your growth is in your hands.

Reactive work revolves around an external locus of control—the customers who are calling you determine your success. It's totally random. Sure, you do good work and provide excellent service, but your sales depend completely on external forces.

Proactive selling is confident selling.

Reactive selling is fearful selling.

Proactive selling lets you determine how much money you will bring home to your family.

Reactive selling volunteers away your control over your future.

Proactive salespeople make more money every year.

Reactive salespeople take home pay that's relatively flat from one year to the next, often for many years at a time.

Proactive salespeople are more positive, bolder, and always happier. They are more successful. They are in control of their lives.

Reactive salespeople feel that things are happening *to* them. They often feel like they are getting taken advantage of by customers. They are not in control.

How to Become Proactive

Most people reading this right now are reactive salespeople.

But here's the wonderful and amazing thing: the way to become a proactive salesperson is to simply decide to make it so.

Decide that you will take control of your sales and extract yourself from the vicious circle of your day.

You will still take calls and incoming orders, of course, but during these calls you will tell customers what else they can buy from you. You will call customers proactively once, twice, or three times a day. You will follow up on quotes and proposals. You will ask for referrals.

Want to become proactive?

Communicate with customers about *more* than what they are calling about.

Help them *more*.

They will be grateful.

You will become proactive.

And your family will enjoy the additional money you bring home.

Selling Boldly	Selling Fearfully
Proactive	Reactive
Confident	Fearful
Boldness	Meekness
Optimistic	Pessimistic
Grateful	Cynical
Consistent Perseverance	Quick Surrenders
Focus on Value and Relationship	Focus on Products and Services
Take Constant Communication Action	Overplan and Underexecute
Make It Look Easy	Laboring, and It Shows
Plan-Driven	Inquiry-Driven

8

Confidence versus Fear

The opposite of fear is confidence.

It should be no surprise that confident salespeople outsell fearful ones.

Confident *humans* outperform fearful ones. At work and also at life.

If you don't feel confident, talk to your happy customers, and ask them what their favorite things are about working with you. They will tell you. And it will be the absolute truth.

Confidence and fear are ways of thinking.

In the next chapter, we discuss boldness and meekness, which are the behavioral manifestations of these ways of thinking. That is, people who think confidently behave boldly, but people who think fearfully behave meekly.

So, how do confident salespeople think differently from fearful sales-people?

In almost every way.

But here are a few of the most important areas:

- The confident salesperson believes the customer is lucky to be hearing from her. The fearful one believes she is lucky the customer picked up the phone.

- The confident salesperson thinks it's highly likely he will get the business, because he is excellent, and the customer knows it. The fearful one thinks it's unlikely he will get the business. He is afraid he will not only miss out on *this* piece of business, but that the customer will fire him if he asks for the business at all.

- The confident salesperson believes the customer *deserves* to benefit from her great value, and that she *owes* it to the customer to offer him additional products, services, and value. But the fearful salesperson believes she is bothering the customer, and does not want to seem needy, or annoying, or pestering. As a consequence, she prefers to stay out of the way.

- The confident salesperson believes there are many additional ways he can help customers beyond what they are buying now. The fearful salesperson thinks that the customer will ask for it if they need to, and so tends to stay out of the way.

- The confident salesperson is driven to provide as much value to the customer as possible. The fearful salesperson's goal is to avoid being yelled at by the customer.

Where Confidence Comes From

Confidence comes from knowing how good you are and behaving accordingly.

Confidence comes from listening to your happy customers speak warmly and positively about you. I teach you how to do this in the next part of this book.

Confidence comes from both a history of success as well as experiencing quick early wins during a new pursuit.

That's one of the defining characteristics of the Selling Boldly program—the wins come quickly.

Twenty percent of did you know questions close and result in a new line item. We know this.

Similarly, 20 percent of quote follow-ups, if implemented the way I lay out in Chapter 29 of this book, will work out successfully.

You will find that customers are quite happy to hear from you when you proactively call them.

Success leads to confidence.

You know what else leads to confidence? A plan!

Instead of bouncing around from one inquiry to the next, having a plan for some fast, simple proactive communications to customers and prospects each day—and then, actually executing on that plan—will give you great confidence.

Use the planners in this book to quickly create your plan.

Like the rest of these mindset shifts, *confidence can be chosen* and then further developed.

Choose confidence.

It pays better.

Selling Boldly	Selling Fearfully
Proactive	Reactive
Confident	Fearful
Boldness	Meekness
Optimistic	Pessimistic
Grateful	Cynical
Consistent Perseverance	Quick Surrenders
Focus on Value and Relationship	Focus on Products and Services
Take Constant Communication Action	Overplan and Underexecute
Make It Look Easy	Laboring, and It Shows
Plan-Driven	Inquiry-Driven

9 | Boldness versus Meekness

The previous chapter covered confidence and fear, which are the thinking precursors to the *behavior* approaches we turn to in this chapter.

You can behave boldly (if you are confident) or you can behave meekly (if you are fearful).

Just like the rest of the mindset shifts we look at in this part of the book, the choice is entirely yours.

It is entirely within your control to choose to behave boldly or meekly. Even if it's uncomfortable, you can choose to be bold—right?

Being meek isn't comfortable, either, but we default to it, don't we? It's not comfortable to cower, but we do it. That's what meekness is, avoiding the action we know we should be doing.

And, unless we are intentional about our mindset, we will find that we tend to behave meekly. That's human nature. We are intensely afraid of rejection and so avoid putting ourselves into situations where it is possible. Do you know where failure is not just possible, and not even probable, but pretty much definite and expected? The *sales profession*. This work demands failure so we can get to the successes. We must work with the customers who say *no* so that we can bring them to the *yes,* and then find the others who will also say *yes.*

Fear is automatic and meekness is automatic.

But confidence and boldness require our active attention and effort to develop.

What Bold People Do

Because boldness is about behavior, bold people simply *do* things differently from meek people.

- **When we are bold, we take more action.** We underplan and overexecute. Because we are confident about our value (we think confidently), we implement multiple communications with customers and prospects without overthinking them. Salespeople who feel meek, on the other hand, are frequently planning and rarely executing. They have meetings, ask for lots of advice, try to make the communication perfect (which it will *never* be) and try to delay action as long as possible. Behaving boldly means taking lots of action. *Ready? FIRE! Aim.* Aim while you fire. See what's working, assess success, and make adjustments. You can't do any of these things before firing! If you try, you're just guessing. Take the action, then make edits if necessary.

- **When we are bold, we pick up the phone.** We don't shy away from it like we do when we are meek. When we are bold, we know our customers are happy to hear from us. When we are meek, we believe we are bothering them and taking up their time. When we are bold, we call customers without an agenda, simply to check and say hello, and to tell them, "I was just thinking about you." (*Nobody* can get mad at you if you tell them you were just thinking about them.) When we are meek we feel that we need a very good and specific reason to call our customers, lest they get mad at us. Bold people know that calling a customer to catch up, when their hair isn't on fire, *is* a good reason to check in with them. Bold salespeople use the phone. Meek salespeople revert to email or other less personal communications pathways. And, frequently, meek salespeople simply *don't communicate at all.* "I don't want to bother the customer," they think. Bold salespeople know they are never a bother, because they offer great value. Meek people don't have a handle on their value, and they are managed by an all-consuming need to avoid rejection, failure, and angering the customers.

- **When we are bold, we ask for the business.** We pivot to the sale. We ask how many the customer would like. We ask the customer how they would like to pay. We ask the customer when they'd like their order delivered. Or when they'd like to meet to kick off the project. We *assume* they want to work with us, because why wouldn't they? They'd be crazy to not want our great value. *Assume they want to work with you and you will usually be right.*

- **When we are bold, we try to help our current customers more, all the time.** We consistently remind them about what else they can buy from us by asking the did you know question. We inquire what else they're buying from the competition, letting them know that *we* would like to help them with these products or services. We let our good customers know that they are among our best customers, and we would like to expand our relationship with them. This is what bold salespeople do. And we can be bold only if we think confidently. Meek salespeople, who think fearfully, are usually afraid to let the customer know about what else they can buy. "I've already told them about this," they think. "If they need it, they'll let me know." This is incorrect because (1) they're busy and you assume they *know* what else they can buy from you, and (2) you assume they'll pick up the phone to call *you.* This is unlikely because if they're not buying it from you *now,* they are probably buying it elsewhere, and will go to *that* provider first. So if you don't tell them—repeatedly—about what else they can buy from you, they will not. But salespeople who are meek avoid the telling part. And they avoid asking what else the customer is buying else-where, because they are afraid the customer will tell them, "It's none of your business!"

- **When we are bold, we ask for referrals**. Because we know that customers love to give referrals. It makes them look good, after all, to refer a friend or a colleague to *you.* And when we are bold, we know that we deserve this referral, and we *want* to help our customer's col-leagues and acquaintances. But when we are meek, we avoid asking for referrals, because we are afraid that the customer will not give us one. We are afraid the customer might like us less than we think. And of course, we don't want to anger the customer by asking for a referral. Bold salespeople know that there is basically no chance that a happy, sat-isfied customer will get mad when we ask them for a referral. But meek salespeople are filled with fear to the point that they *expect* the customer will be mad, and are very pleasantly surprised—every time!—when they do not get angry.

- **When we are bold, we ask a question and remain silent until the customer answers it**, giving her time to think about her answer. When we are meek, we fill the silences with our nervous chatter, because we are afraid we will offend the customer with our silence. We do not realize that while *we* may have been thinking about asking them for a referral for a week, *they* have not been thinking about the referral for us and require some time to think about who they know who would be a good fit. Bold salespeople leverage silence to their advantage so that the customer can volunteer information that the salespeople don't even know to ask about. But this is not possible if you do not offer silence for the customer to think. Meek people do not offer silence. They do not ask the customer to make decisions. They do not give the customer many opportunities to buy.

Meekness is Unfair to the Customer

When we are meek, we are being unfair to the customer.

Customers would like to buy more from you. I know this because they've been with you so long.

They keep coming back.

They *enjoy* working with you. They'd like to do it some more.

But when you are meek, you don't offer them these opportunities.

You don't put yourself in a position to help the customer in the way they want to be helped by you.

You don't ask them for the *yes*.

But you work hard to avoid the *no*.

When you are meek, you are merely existing with a customer.

You are taking orders.

But you are not nurturing the relationship and helping them *more*, which is really all customers want from us.

They want us to be present.

They want us to show them that we care about them.

They want us to *be there* for them.

When you are meek, you are not there for them.

You are doing your customers a disservice.

They don't deserve this from you.

Remember, It's Your Choice

Being bold is better, right?

Well, you can *choose* to behave boldly. Right now, you can choose and begin.

It's up to you.

You know what to do.

And now you know what bold people do.

If you want to be bold, and serve your customers better, and make more money, decide right now to be bold, not meek. To be confident, not afraid.

It's your decision.

Make it!

Selling Boldly	Selling Fearfully
Proactive	Reactive
Confident	Fearful
Boldness	Meekness
Optimistic	Pessimistic
Grateful	Cynical
Consistent Perseverance	Quick Surrenders
Focus on Value and Relationship	Focus on Products and Services
Take Constant Communication Action	Overplan and Underexecute
Make It Look Easy	Laboring, and It Shows
Plan-Driven	Inquiry-Driven

10 | Optimism versus Pessimism

Henry Ford said, "Whether you think you can, or you think you can't, you're right."

This is one of my favorite quotes in the world.

Our behavior follows our thinking.

We *do* what we think.

Our beliefs shape our actions.

So, if you wake up in the morning and believe you're going to have a terrible day, you probably will. You'll be *looking* for it to be terrible. You'll even be taking actions that will help your day be terrible. You'll be actively undermining yourself:

- "Of *course,* there's traffic! What else is new?"
- "My son is going to argue with me, but today I'm going to give it back to him!"
- "I *hate* getting my teeth cleaned at the dentist's—it's going to hurt like crazy."

Now, if you wake up in the morning and believe you're going to have a *good* day, there's a good chance that you will. You will be looking for the upside and opportunity and value in exactly the same experiences. The events won't change one bit, but your *orientation* to them will be totally different, which will change your thinking entirely, which will, of course, affect your behavior and, ultimately, your mood:

- "The extra time in the car will let me listen to that good audio book I've been meaning to get to—or, imagine it!, to call some of my customers proactively and check in with them."
- "When my son pushes back today, it will be a wonderful teaching moment and we'll examine both sides of the issue calmly."
- "I'm not looking forward to the dentist today, but who does? When it's done, my teeth will look great, and I won't have to go again for another six months!"

Exactly the same situations, but a completely different mental approach.

The latter, the optimistic one, identifies the *upside* of each difficult situation you might encounter today. Conversely, the former, pessimistic approach looks at the worst-case scenario of each frustration. Which approach do you think will lead to the better day?

I love the Henry Ford quote because it addresses many of the elements that are required for fast sales growth, and many of the areas that I work on with clients.

Optimism Makes Money

Optimistic salespeople will always outsell pessimistic ones.

If you think you will make the sale before your meeting or phone call, there is a chance that you will.

But if you think you will not make the sale, I will bet my children's college money—which is very important to me—that you will not succeed.

Either way, you're right.

In Martin Seligman's seminal book, *Learned Optimism,* he argues that we can train ourselves to be optimistic. There's a reason he's widely acknowledged as the father of positive psychology. In this case, as in nearly all cases with Seligman, he's exactly right.

I teach salespeople to be more optimistic every day by showing them how happy their customers really are, because—as discussed at length throughout this book—we lose track of how happy our customers are.

They don't tell us and we don't ask—because we're all busy—and we only hear from the customers who are either unhappy or stressed out.

I *see* salespeople and managers and executives becoming more optimistic every day.

I also see the vast majority of them sell more as a result.

Why is optimism so important? Here are the four major reasons:

1. **Optimistic salespeople tend to have an internal locus of control.** That is, *my success is within my control.* To sell more, I can call more customers and prospects, offer them more products and services to buy, and then ask them for some referrals. Conversely, pessimistic salespeople feel there is little they can do, but, rather, that things are happening *to* them: to sell more, we really need to lower our prices and expand our product range. Since that is not within our control as salespeople, we feel that there is nothing we can do to grow sales.

2. **Your approach will reflect your optimism:** you will look for more ways to help your customers more. You will see objections as interests rather than failures. You'll be active, present, and helpful.

3. **Your language, and even your tone, will be positive.** You'll focus on what is possible rather than on what isn't. You'll speak with energy and brightness, which your customers will respond to positively.

4. That's because **people are drawn to optimism and positivity, and are repelled by pessimism and negativity.** We want to do business with people who we like. If I'm the customer, and you make me feel badly every time we talk, I'm going to avoid talking with you, and quickly. On the other hand, if you're a positive and happy person who I enjoy spending time with, I'm going to *look for* opportunities to speak with you!

That's how it works. Buyers who enjoy working with their salespeople look for opportunities to spend more money with them. If you're optimistic, you're enjoyable to be around. If you are pessimistic you are, basically and by definition, unpleasant to be around. And you will be avoided.

How to Be Optimistic

Here are some quick ways to develop optimism:

1. **Regularly think about your wins.** Consider the successes you've had. Our nature is to focus on the failures and the rejections. Those

come with the territory, but we tend to dwell there. Don't. Go over your wins. Think about them. Think about the good work you did. Analyze it. Write it up. Look at it. Enjoy it. Appreciate it.

2. **Be grateful**. We are so lucky. We get to help people! There are prospects and customers who *want* to work with us, and who very much appreciate what we do. *We get to make money by helping people in amazing ways.* That's pretty wonderful.

3. **Listen to your happy customers.** Go through the conversations with customers I lay out in Part III of this book. Ask them what they like best about working with you and then believe them. They're telling you the truth. You're fantastic.

4. **Simply,** *choose* **optimism.** You get to decide every day if you will be optimistic or pessimistic. You even get to decide on every phone call. It's completely in your control.

5. **Think that you can, and you will**. Think that you can't, or won't, and you will not. There's really only one right decision, isn't there? The choice is ours. It's up to us. Choose optimism!

Selling Boldly	Selling Fearfully
Proactive	Reactive
Confident	Fearful
Boldness	Meekness
Optimistic	Pessimistic
Grateful	Cynical
Consistent Perseverance	Quick Surrenders
Focus on Value and Relationship	Focus on Products and Services
Take Constant Communication Action	Overplan and Underexecute
Make It Look Easy	Laboring, and It Shows
Plan-Driven	Inquiry-Driven

11 | Gratitude versus Cynicism

Gratitude is the feeling of conscious appreciation for what we have (in sales, customers), what we get to try to acquire (prospects), and even what we do not have (customers who are not yet working with us, or even those customers who have rejected us).

While *ungrateful* is the opposite of gratitude, I wanted to use a slightly different mindset here as the negative version of gratitude. It's a way of thinking that I see frequently among salespeople who are not proactive or confident or bold—or grateful. This is an approach to life and work by salespeople who are driven heavily by fear: the word is *cynicism*. When I look up the definition of "cynical," I get *distrustful of human sincerity or integrity; concerned only with one's own interest and typically disregard accepted or appropriate standards to achieve them.*

When we are grateful, of course, we appreciate our customers—that's easy and obvious. They pay us. They choose us. We are grateful.

But we also give thanks for prospects who provide us an opportunity to grow every day. *I have a wonderful chance to grow thanks to these prospects.*

But when we are cynical, prospects often frustrate us. *I'm sick of chasing them!*

When we are grateful, we acknowledge the importance of the customers who tell us *no*. They keep us going. We do not give up on them. We try again with them, in different ways, at different times, with different products and services. They need us, and we get to show them this. How lucky are we?

When we are cynical, we do not see the value in people who reject us. We take it personally, of course, when they tell us *no*. We feel that we have wasted time. We wonder why they took the time to meet with us, or even request a quote, if they were just using us to compare to the competition. *They just used us to get a lower price,* we say.

And even when this happens, grateful people will find the positive: *now I know what this person is like. This won't happen again. Good, onward!*

The Power of Gratitude

In his wonderful book, *The Happiness Advantage,* Shawn Achor writes that "Few things in life are as integral to our well-being [as gratitude]. Countless studies have shown that consistently grateful people are more energetic, emotionally intelligent, forgiving, and less likely to be depressed, anxious, or lonely. And it's not that people are only grateful *because* they are happier, either; gratitude has proven to be a significant *cause* of positive outcomes."

How powerful is that?!

How do you think having more energy and being more emotionally intelligent and forgiving will affect your sales?!

What do you think happens to sales when we are less depressed, anxious, or lonely?

That is the immense power of gratitude.

We Can Choose to Be Grateful Right Now

Continuing the theme from the other chapters in this section: you can choose to be grateful—or cynical—right now.

You can decide, at this moment, to live and work and sell gratefully.

It's totally within your control to make this decision.

You simply need to want to be grateful, and then you will!

You *practice* being grateful, too.

In Martin Seligman's book *The Optimistic Child* (which is a must-read if you have young children), he lays out a simple technique for practicing gratitude with kids—and we have been following it for years. Seligman teaches parents to ask their kids this simple question when they are in bed, right before the lights are turned off: "What are three good things that

SELLING BOLDLY	Applying the New Science of Positive Psychology to Dramatically Increase Your Confidence, Happiness, and Sales

▮ THE SELLING BOLDLY MINDSET PLANNER

Date Range:

Three Recent Sales Wins I'm Proud Of
1.
2.
3.

Three Specific Things I'm Grateful For (Personal or Professional)
1.
2.
3.

Top Three Things My Customers Value and Appreciate About Working With Me
1.
2.
3.

Three People (Or Groups of People) Who Deserve For Me To Take Action This Week, Even When It's Difficult
1.
2.
3.

Top Three Perseverance Priorities (I Will Try Again Here This Week)
1.
2.
3.

ALEX • GOLDFAYN
Get digital versions of this and other planners at www.goldfayn.com/Copyright 2018 Alex Goldfayn

happened today?" Sometimes we modify this with our own children to: "What are three things you are grateful about tonight?" Or, "What are three things from today that you love?" The point is to get your children to *think* about positivity and gratitude, in specifics, before they sleep. On many nights it's the last thing they talk about with us that day, then they sleep on it. *We are programming our kids to be grateful.* Seligman writes that his research shows that this early programming inoculates children against depression now and later in life. That's extraordinary!

We can do the same thing in our adult lives also. Take a look at "The Selling Boldly Mindset Planner" here. It's simple and straightforward; it's based on Seligman's three-good-things-at-night, and the research shows this works. And in sales, being grateful will have a huge impact on your success. It will also make you more optimistic, confident, bold, and proactive. The most important nuance with gratitude is to write or think about it *daily*. Multiple times each day is even better. So, make use of the gratitude planner that follows—and download a digital copy at www.Goldfayn.com.

What Salespeople Can Be Grateful For

Here's what we can be grateful for:

- Our customers.
- Our prospects.
- The people who have rejected us.
- Our colleagues.
- Our company.
- Our supportive family.
- This meeting you have coming up.
- The current problem you are working on resolving for this customer.
- That the phone rings *all day* and people want to talk to you and buy from you! Do you know how lucky that is?!
- That you get to let a wonderful customer know what else she can buy, because today she buys only a small percentage of what you have to offer.
- That this terrific customer will have referrals for you, and that you get to ask her for them.
- That your customer is happy to hear from you by phone.

This list can go on for pages.

Use it as a reference when you create your own list in your mindset planner.

We Get to Struggle Here

One last word on gratitude.

If you read my last book, *The Revenue Growth Habit,* or have seen me speak, you probably know that I was born in Ukraine, when it was still part of the former Soviet Union. We had almost nothing when we lived there, and even less when we came here, to America, in 1978. My dad, at the age of 26, dragged the family out of that place to bring us here for a better life. We came with around $20 in U.S. currency, no connections, and no English language. My dad was a trained electrical engineer at the time, but without knowing English, he could not do that work. He came here to chase the American dream, and so that I could chase it too. I was only two years old at the time, but there isn't a day that goes by that I am not aware of how lucky I am to be here.

As salespeople, when we have problems here (and the problems will always come; that's life), we *get to struggle here,* in America. We get to struggle in the most entrepreneurial country in the world where the amount of money we make is determined only by our effort and our perseverance. That is, how hard we *try,* and how hard we *try again.*

It's a privilege to struggle here. We are *lucky* that we get to try to overcome problems *here.*

No matter what your political leanings, or your thoughts about the people who are in elected office today, there is no better place on the planet to overcome obstacles than in America.

Because here, if you put in the work, and you don't give up, you actually *do* overcome obstacles.

In many parts of the world, life doesn't work this way.

And that's a heck of a thing to be grateful for!

Selling Boldly	Selling Fearfully
Proactive	Reactive
Confident	Fearful
Boldness	Meekness
Optimistic	Pessimistic
Grateful	Cynical
Consistent Perseverance	Quick Surrenders
Focus on Value and Relationship	Focus on Products and Services
Take Constant Communication Action	Overplan and Underexecute
Make It Look Easy	Laboring, and It Shows
Plan–Driven	Inquiry–Driven

12 | Perseverance versus Surrender

"Many of life's failures are people who did not realize how close they were to success before they gave up."—Thomas Edison.

To me, this quote means that if you've already been rejected eight times, a ninth rejection is no worse. It's the same. Because, really, what's the difference between eight and nine rejections? Or 12? Pretty much nothing. You still don't have the business—so it certainly hasn't gotten *worse*.

So try again.

Try a different way.

Ask a different question.

Go to a different person, perhaps.

But do not give up.

Let the competition give up.

We don't give up.

We persevere.

The Power of Perseverance

I was speaking at a consulting conference about three years ago, and also speaking that day was Martin Seligman. Now, I am in front of audiences once or twice a week, so I rarely watch other speakers. But when I heard that Seligman would also be speaking, I parked myself in a seat with a good view and sat there, transfixed, hanging on to every word.

Why? Because as I detailed earlier, I studied Seligman in college. He is in the psychology textbooks! In fact, he has been in them for 40 years or longer!

Well, here stood Seligman, a fellow speaker, presenting at the same conference as I was.

Today, as discussed in Chapter 3, he is not only still working and researching but he also runs the Positive Psychology Center at the University of Pennsylvania. He is widely acknowledged as the father of the field of positive psychology, around which the mindset concepts in this book are based. So, Seligman is quite possibly the world's leading authority on happiness, optimism, success, and it turns out, perseverance.

Here is what he said, which is seared into my brain, as though he was saying it only to me, and only yesterday. He said that his research has found again and again that perseverance and resilience—that is, *trying again and not giving up*—is twice as important to success as talent is! Another way of saying this is that perseverance and resilience are two-thirds of the success equation, and talent is only one-third.

Think about the incredible power of this when it comes to selling.

It is why less talented salespeople outperform more talented ones. They try harder. They don't give up. They don't stop at the "no."

This powerful concept is also why we frequently see less talented athletes outperforming more talented ones. We often see less skilled sports players accumulate better statistics and results than their more athletically gifted colleagues. Why is this?

They don't give up.

They persevere.

Because they've always had to.

Meanwhile, gifted athletes have never really had to learn how to keep trying in the face of adversity because they've always succeeded on the strength of their talent. So they don't know what to do when they are not the best on the field anymore, because they have always been successful.

It's the same with salespeople.

Trying again, when the customer says *no,* is everything.

It's Not Our Job to Give Up

After my speeches, audience members frequently ask me to follow up with them to discuss implementing this Selling Boldly program at their organization. One company owner asked me to reach out to him by phone, so over the next several weeks I called. But he was never there, so I left messages with his staff members who answered the phone.

On the fifth or sixth phone call, the man who picked up the phone said to me, "If he doesn't return *this* call, maybe don't call back."

I didn't even hesitate: "I'll talk to you tomorrow," I said.

And I did.

And I connected with him.

And then we met to discuss working together.

And then we *did* work together.

Why?

Because I kept trying to help him and because I didn't give up on him.

It's not my job to give up on somebody who asked me to follow up with him.

Are you kidding me? A highly qualified prospect asked me for help (he spent two hours in a room with me, listening to and considering my approaches, and *then* decided he wanted to have a conversation) and I'm going to stop trying because some guy at his office is tired of taking messages?

That's not the work. Giving up is not the work.

It's not my job to give up on him.

It's not your job to quit on your prospects. They deserve your great value.

It's not your job to give up on trying to help your customers and prospects more.

That's not the work.

The work is continuing to try to help.

Persevering in the Face of Adversity

As I touched on in Part I, I have had entire years in my business when every single *client* had told me *no* previously. Some of my best clients actually spent years rejecting me. But I don't take rejection personally, and I don't blame myself for it, ever.

Many years ago, a business coach taught this: the prospect is the buyer; their job is to buy. If they didn't buy, they didn't do their job! That's not my problem; that's their problem. And it's certainly not my fault that they're not ready to buy! I'm fully aware of the value I offer to my clients. My clients add 10 to 20 percent to their sales annually by implementing my concepts. I know what I do and I know what I can do for my customers.

And it's certainly not *your* fault that this prospect did not buy. You've done your job. You've laid out the value. You've presented the great improvements the prospect would experience with you. If they're not ready to buy it at this moment, our job is to give customers another moment! That's all. Keep trying. Because that's our job. That's the work.

Perseverance will make you a lot of money.

In fact, if you look back over your important sales with your company, and think through the process that led you to the sales, you will probably find that many of these important customers probably said *no* before they said *yes*. And if you didn't persevere, you would have never closed these sales.

My Children's Trees

When my children were born, my wife and I planted two beautiful maple trees in our backyard, one for each of them. One of the trees turns a beautiful deep red color in the fall (that one is Noah's tree) and one is a Crimson King, which is deep purple all year long (that's Bella's tree). Our hope was that the branches and leaves from these trees could be used in important moments during our children's lives, like their weddings, for example.

About three years ago we moved.

We bought our new house, moved in, and then put the old house on the market.

Well, I needed to get the trees to the new house.

We had found a buyer for the house and the closing was in 30 days.

I *thought* that a few guys could come with shovels and simply dig up the trees.

But to my surprise, everybody I talked to told me this was not possible. The trees were too big. They had been in the ground for about five years at that point.

What I needed, they said, was a hydraulic tree spade.

What is a hydraulic tree spade, you may ask?

A huge truck, about the size and shape of a cement mixer, that uses four giant high-power spades to dig up big trees, root ball and all, and load them onto the back of the truck in one fell swoop.

This sounded promising, but only about a dozen or so companies in the Chicago area have such a truck.

I started calling them.

And they started rejecting me.

These people do parking lots, golf courses, and parkways.

They don't do two little backyard trees.

I called the first six, and they all said sorry, no.

They advised me to buy a couple of new trees instead! That's right: these companies whose job it was to move trees, told me to just buy some trees instead.

I called the next few; they also declined.

Now my parents are also telling me I should just buy some new trees.

But I wanted *these* trees. They were important to me, and totally sentimental. They were my children's trees!

One provider agreed to move my trees on Saturday morning, but *emailed* me on Friday night to say that he couldn't make it.

I called the last remaining company, and they said, *Sorry, no.*

At this point, my wife was also saying I should give up on this and just get a couple of other trees.

I *could* have bought an entire forest of trees for the prices these people charged, but that's another conversation!

By now, the closing was in a few days, and I was getting desperate.

I wanted *my children's* trees.

And I had already been rejected by a dozen companies. That's right: a dozen companies refused to take my money. The job was too small.

So I started calling companies in Wisconsin, just north of the state border from where we lived.

Five more calls; and five more rejections.

On the sixth effort, two days before the closing, I found a guy!

He agreed to move the trees the next day.

He grabbed them, intact root ball and all, one at a time and transported them to the new house. On the afternoon before our closing on the old house, the new trees were placed in the ground on our front lawn, in a space that is close to both the sidewalk and the street so everybody who walks by can enjoy the children's trees.

As the driver was planting the trees at our new home, my wife and I stood watching.

And she said to me, "I don't know anybody else who would have persevered enough to get *these* trees here."

And this is the kind of perseverance that sales success requires.

I had already been rejected a dozen times.

So, the next five rejections were no worse.

After two or three rejections, the ensuing rejections leave you in *exactly the same position* you were in before.

It's no worse.

So if it's important—and helping more customers more is *always* important—keep trying.

Do not quit.

We owe it to the customer to keep trying.

They deserve that from us.

We owe it to our families to try to bring home more money.

They deserve it.

We owe it to ourselves.

You deserve the additional revenue.

You work hard, provide tremendous value, and your customers are generally very happy with your work.

You deserve more revenue.

Go get it.

Keep trying.

Keep trying to help people.

And never, ever, give up.

Selling Boldly	Selling Fearfully
Proactive	Reactive
Confident	Fearful
Boldness	Meekness
Optimistic	Pessimistic
Grateful	Cynical
Consistent Perseverance	Quick Surrenders
Focus on Value and Relationship	Focus on Products and Services
Take Constant Communication Action	Overplan and Underexecute
Make It Look Easy	Laboring, and It Shows
Plan-Driven	Inquiry-Driven

13 | Value and Relationship versus Products and Services

As part of nearly every revenue growth project that I do with clients, I speak to their customers. I've done thousands of these customer interviews over the past decade or so. As I'll detail in the next part of this book, I ask the customers what they like best about working with my clients. They talk to me about things like reliability, dependability, how my client saves them time, helps them make money, and helps them sleep at night. What they *do not* talk about at all are the products and services! Or the problems! Or the price!

We love to talk about the products and services. We detail them, we present them, we discuss the specifications, we talk about the installation, or the implementation. We stay focused on the *stuff*.

But the customer doesn't think about your products and services when they think about you. They think about the *value of buying those products and services from YOU*.

The products and services are a commodity.

The products and services are *boring!* Your *stuff* is not exciting.

Buying it from *you*—that's what excites the customer.

It's your relationship that keeps them coming back.

Yes, the products are important.

But as one customer told me recently in an interview for a client: "We *buy* the product, but we go to *them* for the relationship. It's the friendship that keeps us coming back."

They can buy it anywhere, and they know it. They often tell me this.

They can buy it cheaper than they do from you, elsewhere, and they know it. They often tell me this.

So, it's not what you sell, it's how buying it from *you* makes your customers feel.

That's what they focus on. That's what they talk about.

But it's not what *you* focus on when you talk with your customers, is it?

Focusing on Value versus Products and Services

Confident, bold, proactive salespeople focus on their value when talking to the customer. Here are the kinds of things these salespeople emphasize when they call on their customers and prospects:

- You are easy to reach.
- You are always available.
- You will ship orders on time, when you say you will.
- If you come across a problem—and from time to time it's possible there will be problems—you will always be up front with the customer and tell them in advance.
- You won't leave them in a lurch. You won't *hide* problems from them.
- Many times, you've put the product in your own car, and driven it to your customers.
- Your customer is your priority. You look out for them.
- Your customers tell you that you are reliable, dependable, and easy to work with. (I like to use, "My customers tell me that . . . " here, because it's true, and also because it's a bit awkward to say, "I'm easy to work with." If I'm the customer, I may be thinking, "Sure buddy, sure you are.")
- You use silence to let the customer think and speak.

Conversely, if you are fearful, meek, and pessimistic, you focus pretty much entirely on the product:

- You repeat the product name a lot.
- You lay out the features and specifications for the majority of your time with the customer.
- You talk about installation and usage.
- If you sell services, you spend a lot of time discussing your process.
- You talk about pricing, and tend to focus on it.
- You do a lot of the talking, because you are not confident in your value and ability to help this customer.

Now, you be the customer. Which of these two approaches would you prefer? Which one would feel better to you?

Of course, the former is far more desirable by customers than the latter.

And, thankfully, the former happens to grow your sales far better than the latter!

How Do You Know What Your Value Is?

How do you know what value to focus on?

The answer is simple: ask your customers. They'll tell you.

And they'll be happy to do so.

In Part III, I give you scripts and language to do so.

Focus on your value. Customers prefer it.

And it sells better.

Selling Boldly	Selling Fearfully
Proactive	Reactive
Confident	Fearful
Boldness	Meekness
Optimistic	Pessimistic
Grateful	Cynical
Consistent Perseverance	Quick Surrenders
Focus on Value and Relationship	Focus on Products and Services
Take Constant Communication Action	Overplan and Underexecute
Make It Look Easy	Laboring, and It Shows
Plan-Driven	Inquiry-Driven

14

Taking Constant Communication Action versus Overplanning and Underexecuting

Doing Things versus Thinking About Doing Them

Sometimes when I'm teaching client workshops—with their customer-facing teams, including sales and customer service people—and I'm reviewing a sales technique like asking for referrals, someone raises a hand (usually an outside salesperson) and says, "Oh, I ask for referrals all the time."

And then the conversation goes like this, almost always:

Me: "That's great! Let's talk about that. Tell me about the referrals."

Salesperson: "My customers are really happy, so they give me a lot of referrals."

Me: "That's great! How many would you guess?"

Silence.

Me: "In a week, how many referrals would you say you get like this?"

Salesperson: "Two or three." Then: "At least one."

Me: "That's great! So about four a month?"

Salesperson: "Yeah. Probably one or two a month."

103

Me: "Okay. And when you get these referrals, are they coming in organically, or are you asking for them?" [Remember, this salesperson jumped in to say he asks for referrals all the time.]

Silence.

Nodding.

Silence.

Salesperson: "I guess they're just coming in."

Me: "That means you're doing great work, and I'm not surprised because I talked to your customers before this workshop started. But I think I'm hearing you say that you don't ask for these referrals?"

Salesperson: "No, I guess I don't."

So what happened here?

This salesperson *thought* he often asked for referrals.

But when we talked about it for a minute, he realized he did not.

Why did he think he asked for lots of referrals? (He was not lying when he made his statement. He actually *believed* he asked for referrals frequently.)

Here's what happened:

Like many salespeople, *he confused thinking about doing something with actually doing it.*

Most salespeople *think* they make a quantity of proactive phone calls, but they do not. They think they make a lot of calls because they *know* they should use the phone more, and they think about doing it a great deal, but they don't actually do it. They think about it so much that they begin to believe they actually do make a number of proactive calls.

Most salespeople know they should ask for the sale frequently. They think about it often, but they do not do it nearly as much. And yet, if you ask most salespeople if they pivot to the sale often, they will tell you yes, they do. But they do not. They merely think about it.

It's the same with referrals. And testimonials. And calling on enough prospects who are not yet customers. And sending a useful, high-value newsletter to a good list.

We *think* about these things a lot. So much so that we begin to believe that we do them.

But in reality, we do not.

It's a defense mechanism our brain uses to protect ourselves from self-criticism, which leads to anxiety and depression.

If we believe we do it already, then there's no need to pressure ourselves further, and there's certainly no reason to beat ourselves up. Because we're already doing it, right?

No, we're not.

Be honest with yourself.

Are you *actually* executing enough of the proactive communications I've talked about (and discuss in more detail in the coming chapters)?

Or are you just spending time *thinking* about them, but not necessarily doing them?

We Need Action, Not Perfection

Sales growth requires short, quick, crisp action.

We must communicate.

We must *not* attempt to perfect these communications.

Perfection leads almost directly to procrastination. In fact, they are basically one and the same.

Taking action is different than meeting about it.

Or planning it for weeks.

Taking action means you have to make the communications.

Because while the products or services need to be perfect, or close to perfect, the communications do not.

They merely need to be helpful.

So, make your communications.

Talk to customers and prospects, all the time.

Take action.

Spread your value far and wide.

Selling Boldly	Selling Fearfully
Proactive	Reactive
Confident	Fearful
Boldness	Meekness
Optimistic	Pessimistic
Grateful	Cynical
Consistent Perseverance	Quick Surrenders
Focus on Value and Relationship	Focus on Products and Services
Take Constant Communication Action	Overplan and Underexecute
Make It Look Easy	Laboring, and It Shows
Plan–Driven	Inquiry–Driven

15

Making It Look Easy versus Laboring

Sometimes it's not easy.

We wake up in the morning, and we just don't have it. We don't feel like it. We're not up to the grind. We do not roll out of bed our usual happy selves, eager to face the day.

Sometimes, we go to the office and do not look forward to picking up the phone. We do not look forward to all of the phone calls that will come in. We know we will need to address problems and urgent issues, but it's not in us on this day. We're not feeling it.

But even on these days, even when it's hard, we must make it look easy.

Have you ever been at a restaurant with your family, where the waiter or waitress was really laboring?

You try to get them over to your table, and they run past you, carrying their tray, telling you they'll be right with you.

You wait a little longer, and raise your hand.

The server says it'll be another minute as they scurry past.

Finally, they arrive at your table, breathless.

Sweat is on their brow.

They let out a big sigh, right in front of you (right *on* you), and ask, "Okay, what can I get you?"

No!

Get out of here with that stress!

Nobody wants stress in a restaurant, when you are trying to relax with your family.

Nobody is paying you to show how stressed you are and how hard you're working.

Conversely, people will pay good money to be around people who make them feel good.

If you can get your customers to believe that when they work with you, good things are *possible* because of your positive attitude and approach, they will keep coming back. Because people are drawn to positivity. We want to surround ourselves with people who we want to spend more time with, and people who make us feel good.

Putting your *hard effort* on display does the opposite of this.

It saps people's energy, and ultimately repels people.

Even when it's hard, make it look easy.

Because that's what people want.

How to Make It Look Easy

But if it's not fun, or you're not in the mood, or you just don't want to deal with this person right now, how do you make it look easy?

Here are some techniques.

Be grateful anyway. Even if it's hard work, spend 10 seconds thinking about what there is to be grateful for:

- This customer is paying money to work with *you,* how cool is that?! They could be buying from anyone, but they have selected *you.*
- You're going to help this customer a great deal today. You do work that improves lives and companies. *That* is amazing.
- If you help this customer, you are also helping your company a great deal. You are generating a sale, or a more satisfied customer. This benefits the company tremendously.
- As such, you are helping all of the staff members in the firm. They too shall benefit from the results you are creating.

■ Your family benefits too. A new sale means more money for your family. A problem solved likely means a future sale in the near term. You're helping provide for your family.

Think about your who and your why. Why do you do this work? Who do you do it for? Do these people deserve your best, most positive effort? The answer is probably yes, so give the people what they deserve.

Be Optimistic. Always remember that this is a choice, and you get to make it. *I just don't feel like it today,* is a thought just as, *I'm going have a fantastic day* is. You get to decide. What will your position be? Will you move through the day thinking, *"Even though I don't have my best 'stuff' today, I'll do my best to help my customers anyway,"* or will you spend the day thinking, *"I hate this."* The first thought is righteous, and of incredible value to you and your productivity. The second thought is a killer. In fact, as I wrote, *"I hate this,"* I could *feel* the negativity that this creates in my belly. Can you feel it? If *you* are thinking that you hate it, the *customer* can feel that! Even though you are not telling the customer you hate it, *they can feel it.* Don't let your customers feel that, and don't let them see you working hard.

Smile. Sounds corny, I know. But people can *hear* your smile. In fact, make yourself laugh during the interaction. Make a joke. Enjoy a light moment with your customer. If there isn't one, create one. If you lighten up, the customer will too.

Find joy. Figure out what's *fun* about this hard work. Is it helping people? Is it making money? Is it setting the right example for your kids, who watch everything you do? Maybe it's that drink you're going to have when this day is over—or that very dinner we discussed earlier in this chapter. Find the fun.

People appreciate ease.

When I talk to the customers of my clients, they often talk about how much they appreciate that it's *easy* to work with you.

Make it easy.

Make it fun.

The customer will feel that.

And they'll keep coming back to you for more of it.

Selling Boldly	Selling Fearfully
Proactive	Reactive
Confident	Fearful
Boldness	Meekness
Optimistic	Pessimistic
Grateful	Cynical
Consistent Perseverance	Quick Surrenders
Focus on Value and Relationship	Focus on Products and Services
Take Constant Communication Action	Overplan and Underexecute
Make It Look Easy	Laboring, and It Shows
Plan-Driven	Inquiry-Driven

16

Plan-Driven versus Inquiry-Driven

Fearful salespeople tend to not have a plan.

They can't predict or forecast their sales very well, nor can they predict with real accuracy which behaviors will lead to new sales.

Worse, they are at the utter mercy of what's incoming.

Maybe a big order will come in.

Or maybe a small one will.

But maybe customers with problems will call all day long, and on this day or this week, you'll sell very little.

Fearful salespeople are afraid because their success is not within their control.

In fact, whether they sell or not has very little to do with what they actually do!

If an incoming caller needs a certain quantity of a particular product, that, and that alone, is what will be sold.

The salesperson is fearful because he is not in charge of what's happening.

In fact, the salesperson is fearful because he often feels like things are careening out of control, from one incoming inquiry to the next.

This book addresses this terrible and painful issue.

This book lets you take back control.

It puts *you* in charge of your success.

Want to sell more? Use the planning tools and systems in this book.

Want to sell more? Follow the simple instructions here to move from reactive selling to proactive selling.

Want to sell more? Do more of the activities in this book.

I don't need hours each day from you.

I'm not even asking you for half an hour.

I just need a few minutes a day.

Can you find a few minutes each day to make more money to take home your family?

Because that's my goal here: to help you make more money.

You deliver incredible value to your customers.

You deserve to make more money. And your family deserves all the good things that this money can buy.

Want to sell more? Spend a little bit of time planning your sales, and be more proactive in communicating with customers and prospects.

In this book I teach you exactly what to do. And even though you probably already know most of what's here, as we discussed earlier there is a difference between knowing what to do and actually doing it.

Selling Boldly is about doing what you already know.

It's about communicating more with people who can buy from you.

It's about helping your customers and prospects more.

This work is positive and pleasant.

You'll find that your customers and prospects will be happy to hear from you, because they're likely not hearing much from your competition.

You'll find your customers and prospects rewarding your effort with new purchases.

The work is joyful and enjoyable.

The work brings quick wins and nearly instant gratification.

The work is not difficult. At all.

It doesn't require much time.

It doesn't cost a penny to do.

The work, quite simply, needs to get done.

Selling Boldly is about making sure you do the work.

I lay out the work in detail in Part IV, with scripts and step-by-step guidelines.

I give you the tools to plan your communications.

And then I'm going to ask you to *do the work.*

It's time to do the work.

It's time to sell more.

It's time to bring more money home to your family.

PART

III

How to Develop the Selling Boldly Mindset

17

Why Feedback from Happy Customers Is the Key to Developing the Selling Boldly Mindset

There is a single activity that will move your mindset from the fearful side of the mindset table to the Selling Boldly side.

There is *one* thing that will move you from reactive to proactive; from fearful to confident; from meek to bold; from pessimistic to optimistic; from cynical to grateful; from giving up to persevering; from focusing on your products and services to focusing on your value and relationship; from overplanning to overexecuting; from laboring to making it look easy; from being inquiry-driven to being plan-driven.

One activity can do all that?

Yes, it is like magic.

It's so effective—like steroids for sales—that it should be illegal.

But it's perfectly legal, your customers will love it, and it will infuse joy and happiness into your life. And then the money comes.

This activity is: proactively talking to your happy customers about what they enjoy and appreciate about working with you, in a systematic and intentional way.

I am not talking about Internet surveys, which many customers accurately perceive to be a demand or a drain on their time.

I am not talking about "Would you answer a few questions for us by email?" which is lazy and also an imposition on the customer.

No, I am talking about a 5- to 10-minute conversation with customers who you *know* are happy, and to dig into exactly what they are happy about.

Why Happy Customers Don't Call

We only hear from customers when they need something or when there is a problem—and most often they aren't in a happy state when they call. Our day is spent addressing urgent matters, frequently from people who are upset or angry. And *every* day is spent this way.

We lose sight of the fact—almost completely—that the majority of our customers are quite happy with us.

In fact, the people who call and complain and issue urgent requests are only around 10 percent of all our customers.

The rest are doing business as usual.

The rest are pleased.

The rest don't call because everything is going well. And they are busy. So they are quietly enjoying your good work.

They're good. There is no need to call.

Humans are wired to complain proactively. The unhappy customers make themselves known. The customers with an urgent need *must* call because of their (usually self-inflicted) time concerns.

But we are not wired to compliment proactively.

A customer will not, for example, call you for the sole purpose of communicating what a wonderful job you are doing, and how you are growing their sales, and how you are reliable, always available, and save them time. That doesn't happen, right? Even though you *do* those things for those customers, they do not proactively pick up the phone to tell you that. Why not? *Because it's assumed that it should be so.* When customers are happy, you are doing what you should be doing. So there's no need to talk.

What Happens When We Talk Only to Unhappy Customers

When we spend days talking with customers who only have problems or urgent needs, our thinking and approach take on the characteristics listed on the right side of our mindset table at the start of every chapter in Part II:

- We become **reactive,** because the phone never stops ringing. There is no end to the problems we must solve.

- We behave **fearfully,** because we believe our customers are unhappy. The phone keeps ringing, and the person on the other end is going to be unhappy. Again.

- We are **meek** in our behavior. Nobody is happy!

- We become **pessimistic.** *This* one is going to be just like the rest! Here we go again!

- We view the world somewhat **cynically.** These people are never happy!

- We persevere less and are **quick to surrender.** We are beaten down.

- We **focus on products and services,** because we are not aware of our great value.

- We tend to underexecute, because we know the outcome that awaits us: unhappy customers!

- The work is hard. **We are laboring and it shows.** Getting yelled at and putting out fires all day is unpleasant.

- Our days and our work lives are determined by who is calling us and what they want. **We are inquiry-driven.** We are not in control.

That's the impact on mindset, and you can imagine what all this does to sales results. Because you are reactive and fearful and meek and pessimistic, you do not offer additional products or services to current customers. You do not ask for the business. You do not pick up the phone to check in with customers proactively. You figure that if they need something more or want to talk to you, they will call. This is not true, of course. They will not call. They are busy. They are not thinking about you and your offerings. *You* are, all day long, but they are *not*. And so, *we* must offer the customers additional products. *We* must be present. *We* must follow up on quotes and proposals. *We* must ask who else our customer works with who also buys our kind of stuff. But we don't. Because we approach the world with the attitudes just detailed. Because we only answer the phone and solve problems. That's what we do. And if the right inquiries come in, we might grow. And if they do not, we will not. And we are totally at the mercy of what's incoming. It's not a good way to live.

What Talking to Happy Customers Does to Us

How do you *solve* all this?

Talk to your happy customers proactively—quickly, but regularly.

Why is this important?

It is not only the antibiotic for all the issues just detailed, but it's also more than that: *it is the fuel that drives the thinking and behaviors that sales growth requires.*

They will tell you what you do for them and how you help them.

They will tell you why they value you.

They will tell you that you are one of their best suppliers.

They will tell you how you save them time, and make them look good to their boss and to their customers.

And because we don't hear this kind of feedback through the course of our normal, reactive day, we are greatly moved and affected by this feedback.

When the salespeople at my clients' companies hear this positive feedback, they are shocked. I do these customer interviews *for* my clients as part of the project, then I play them back for the customer-facing staff.

What happens first is awe. "Wow," they say, with raised eyebrows.

Then comes pride. "It feels good to hear this," they say.

Next, as we debrief and discuss every call, comes this all-important realization to each one in the group: "I'm really helping them. I didn't know they were *this* happy."

Finally, the Holy Grail: "I guess I'm better than I think!"

Ding ding!

I'm speaking directly to you now, the reader of this line at this moment: *you ARE better than you think. Your customers are happier with you than you know. You do amazing work and 90 percent of your customers are quite pleased. That's why they've been with you for so long.* I'm a thousand percent right about this. This is fact and truth and it's indisputable.

But me telling you this is quite different from actually hearing it from your own paying customers, right?

When I say it, you can disagree and push back. Because your experience over the years has informed you otherwise.

But when a customer says it, it's the absolute truth.

Why would they lie?

We're not paying them to tell us these nice things.

They're paying us *and* they're saying them.

And so, these proactive conversations with happy customers—which I will script and detail for you in the next chapter—accomplish the following:

- The cementing of our value **makes us proactive** rather than reactive.

- Hearing the detail and nuance of how we help our customers, in their own voices and words, **skyrockets our confidence.**

- As such, **we become bolder.** We become proactively, systematically bold. How great is that?! How can sales *not* grow?

- We **become optimistic.** My customers really appreciate me!

- We **feel gratitude** for *these* customers, and we want to help them more. We are also grateful for the opportunity to make *other* customers this happy.

- We **grow sales with perseverance.** Once we are aware of our great value, we don't want to keep it from people. We start to believe it is our *duty* to help others like this, and a *no* from a customer simply means *not at this moment.* It is also a mistake by them, because why would they not want to benefit from our tremendous value? So we give them additional moments to say *yes.*

- We **focus on our value and our relationships,** because that is what our customers talk about. They do *not* talk about our products and services when we ask them about what they like best about working with us. The products and services are commodities. They work with us because of *us.* We know where our value is. *It's in what we do, not what we sell.*

- **We make it look easy, even when it's hard.** We are lighter on our feet. We are happier. We find more joy in the work. When there are problems, we do not perceive them as permanent. Sales is not life or death anymore. It's just helping people. That's the work. That's what we do. And now you know.

- **We make quick plans and implement them.** We know what our proactive communications will be this week and we implement them. We know how we will infuse proactivity into our otherwise reactive day.

Just Ask, and They Will Tell You

Have you ever asked somebody for an opinion, and received a response like, "No, I'd rather not tell you what's on my mind!"

Me neither!

People *love* telling others what they think and feel.

And so, ask a customer what he or she likes best about working with you—because you're trying to improve and you'd like to double down on the areas that are working well for them—and they will talk to you for an hour, if you let them. This has been my experience over the past decade or so doing this work.

I've heard the following responses from the customers of my clients *many* times:

- "Wow, thank you for including me!"
- "This call is an example of what I love about them so much. They care!"
- "They are the *last* company that I work with that should be doing this. They're great! The others need to know more about what I'm thinking!"

It's almost like *they* are doing *us* the favor, right?

People *appreciate* being asked.

They're grateful for the opportunity to tell you what is great about you!

As it turns out, people love to give testimonials!

All we have to do is ask.

If we ask, they will tell us.

It's just that we don't ask.

So they don't tell.

Today, we start asking!

18

How to Get Testimonials from Your Happy Customers

This chapter lays out the process of gathering powerful feedback, insights, and testimonials from your happy customers. The foundation for this approach is detailed in my previous book, *The Revenue Growth Habit,* but you will find the details that follow to be a streamlined, updated version of that process. I've personally conducted and overseen thousands of additional customer interviews since writing that book, and the approaches detailed in this chapter take into account the many lessons learned from those sessions.

The Purpose of These Conversations

Always remember the purpose of these conversations: we want testimonials that detail what your customers love about working with you. I know you will be uncomfortable asking for this because we are not used to asking for positive feedback. In fact, it is much more comfortable for us to ask, "What can we do better?" rather than "What do you like best about working with us?"

If it's feedback for improvement, we know what to do. We can jump into action. We go fix the problem.

If it's feedback about what you're doing well, we don't know what to do. A few thoughts about this.

First, you don't have to necessarily *do* anything. You simply have to *understand* and *believe* the positive feedback they are communicating to you.

Second, if you *must do* something, here are a few actions that can help grow your sales:

- Double down on the things your customers say they love about you. For example, if the customer explains that they love it when you come and see them—*see them some more.*
- Next, put their testimonials on paper and keep them on the top of your desk. Read them. Regularly.
- Third, communicate these testimonials to other customers and prospects. This is your key sales growth strategy with this feedback, and I detail it in depth in Chapter 30.

But always remember the *reason* for these conversations—the *why*: we are trying to understand and amass details on what our customers enjoy, value, and appreciate about working with us. That's the work.

First, We Need the Happy Customers

Angry customers do not give good testimonials.

That's why we must set up these conversations with happy customers, the ones who have been with you a long time and keep coming back every year.

The unhappy customers call, right?

They make themselves known and do not require much proactive effort.

We don't need to be intentional about talking to customers with problems. That's a reactive occurrence; those phone calls come to us.

It's the happy customers we need to go get. So, let's go get them.

First, identify a handful you will target.

Happy Customers I Will Ask For Feedback
1.
2.
3.
4.
5.

This Is a Telephone Activity

I cannot emphasize this strongly enough: the customer feedback we are talking about is *not* an Internet survey.

It is not a questionnaire to email.

Those have a place, as a low-level, low-response data-gathering exercise. But this is not one of those.

This is a high-level human conversation focused on value, relationship, and emotion.

This is a telephone activity.

On the phone you can follow up and dig in.

On the phone you can hear your customer's tone of voice and react accordingly.

On the phone you can use silence to your advantage (more on this further on). With emails, the only silence you'll experience is from the customers who don't reply.

On the phone you can respond to what the customer is saying in real time.

On the phone you can listen interactively ("Yes, it's important" or "That's interesting").

You can check for understanding: "Did I get that right?" You can confirm things.

You can even *state the testimonial* yourself and ask if it's true! Here is an example:

You: "So am I hearing you say that working with us saves you time?"

Customer: "Yes, it definitely does."

And here is your testimonial: "Working with T-Co. saves us time."

None of this happens by email.

In fact, little of any real value happens by email. Use the phone instead.

How to Ask for Participation

Here's something that has not changed from when I wrote about this in *The Revenue Growth Habit* three years ago: there are still only two ways to request this kind of customer feedback:

The first option: schedule phone calls to interview your happy customers.

You may schedule the call by email, but it must be conducted by phone. Here is your language to set up the call:

> We're trying to improve our service, and I'm wondering if you'd spend 10 minutes or so giving me some feedback about our work. We'd like to serve you even better, and we are asking only our best customers. You're obviously on the short list. I'd love your take, so that I can serve you even better. Does Tuesday or Thursday at 1 P.M. work for you? Again, I'd need only 10 minutes.

What happy customer in their right mind would say no to this? *No, I'm not going to help you serve me better!*

You will find the vast majority of people agreeing.

The second option: ask for feedback at the end of another conversation.

This is the second option, but in the years since writing this process up in *The Revenue Growth Habit,* I've found this approach to be less effective. Mostly because some salespeople I've worked with find the transition to the testimonial conversation difficult. My best advice here is to just read the conversation request that follows. Read it confidently, joyfully, conversationally, and the customer will be happy to oblige.

The approach here is to initiate the testimonial conversation at the end of another call, where you are discussing something else. Here's what you say:

Okay, are we good on that topic? You're happy? Great, listen, if you have five more minutes, I'd love to get your feedback on how we're doing. I'd like to serve you even better, and I'm asking only my best customers. You're obviously on the short list. Do you have five minutes?

Then transition into the setup that follows.

How to Conduct the Interviews

So, you've got the call on your calendar, the happy customer is expecting your call, and you are calling at the appointed time. Here is what you do.

Set Up the Call

> "Thanks for talking with me, Sally. I appreciate your time. What we're trying to do is improve our service to our good customers, so we're asking for your thoughts, your feedback, and your take on working with us. I'm doing this with only our best customers, and you're on that short list. I'll ask you some specific questions, we'll talk for 10 minutes or so, and then I'll get you off the phone. Does that sound okay?"

Let's quickly analyze what's happening here.

I am asking for testimonials without using the word. "Will you give me a testimonial?" is stressful. That word causes people anxiety. Avoid it.

I am asking for testimonials by asking the customer for feedback. Feedback and reactions are easy. People love being asked what they're thinking. But ask somebody to give you a testimonial and they'll clam up and tell you they have to put their thoughts together and get back to you.

I am making a promise: this will be quick (10 minutes) and easy. I will keep this promise. And if the customer is giving good, long answers, I will make sure to tell the customer a few minutes before time runs out that we are approaching the limit, and that I want to be respectful of their time. The vast majority of responses will be, "That's okay. We can go over," or "Let's take as long as you need." Why do they do this? Because they're enjoying the conversation! It's fun, pleasant, and highly unusual. They don't do this every day! (Or even once a year, in most cases!)

I compliment them repeatedly. In the email and in the first 30 seconds I tell the customer that she is one of our best. People love that. They say, "Thank you." Or, "Oh, wow!" Or, "Well, I hope I won't disappoint you!" Think about that: they are doing *us* a favor. They are giving *us* testimonials. And they are thanking *us* for it!

Now, Get Permission to Record the Call

> " . . . we'll talk for 10 minutes or so, and then I'll get you off the phone. Does that sound okay?"
>
> They will say yes. There is no other answer here.
>
> Then you ask, "Is it okay with you if I record the call?"

The key here is that this is an easy *yes*.

You've set up what you're going to do. You've gained agreement for the structure of the call. You have what I call "yes momentum" at this point. And now you ask if you can record the call. Out of thousands of calls like this, I can think of only two or three people who said no.

If you'd prefer, you can expand the request slightly: "Is it okay with you if I record the call, so that I correctly get what you say?"

The Single Most Important Question

Now that the interview has officially started, and your 10-minute timer has begun, here is the only question you really need.

> What are some of your favorite things about working with us?

This is a big wide-open question, on purpose. Ask, and be quiet. Ask, and listen. The person will likely pause to consider your question, because they've probably never been asked this question before. Ever!

The customer will rattle off a few good areas for us to dig into. For example:

- You're great. You're always on time.
- I can always reach somebody.
- You do what you say you're going to do.

Consider these three different spools of thread.

Now, the Work is to Pull the Thread

Now we must pull the thread to unwind the spool. That is, we want details. One at a time, dig in with some of the following questions:

- Thank you very much for that terrific compliment. Can we dig into these? Tell me about being on time. How? When?
- I'm glad to hear you can always reach somebody. Is that different with your other suppliers?
- What do you mean we do what we say? Can you give me an example?

So, we're just having a conversation, right?

Ask a lot of these types of questions:

- How?
- Why?
- In what way?
- Why did you say that?
- Tell me about that . . .

Then, practice some active listening:

- Interesting . . .
- Huh . . .
- I like that . . .
- Ooh . . .
- What?!
- Wow!
- Really?

Be present.

We're just having a conversation.

If you're talking to your old friend and they tell you their daughter has picked a college, you don't immediately change the topic to the weather. Or yesterday's baseball scores. No, you dig into the daughter's decision:

- Wow, that's great! How did she pick that school?
- How far is that from home?
- What other schools did she consider?
- How do *you* feel about this?
- Does she have any idea what she's going to study yet?

It's the same with the happy customer. Dig into the major topics they provide you.

Now, Pivot to the Value

Now that you have the specific areas the customer finds valuable, it's time to dig into what this does for them:

When we do this, how does that help you?

When we always deliver on time, how does that help you?

What gets better for you, John, when we do this?

These questions can be used on their own, or in combination with one another.

You can ask them in succession. Ask one, let the customer answer, then ask the next.

These are really powerful questions.

Here you are leading the customer to the actual benefit of working with you.

The customer will tell you incredibly high-impact statements like:

- Working with you helps me look good to my customers.
- You help me make my customers happy.
- You let me focus on other parts of my job.
- You save me time.
- You make me more productive.
- You keep me from being yelled at!
- You're reliable.
- You bring me peace of mind.

These are the things that come up again and again in the thousands of interviews I have done with my clients' customers. These are powerful statements of value and relationship. They are about what you do and how you do it, not what you sell. They are about your value, not your products and services. They are about why the customer buys from you. They are about your relationship, not your products. This is what you do. This is how you help people. Believe it.

Other Questions to Ask During the Interview

Here are some other questions to ask during your conversation:

> Does working with us save you time?
> Does working with us save you money?
> Does working with us *make* you money?
> How would you describe us to a colleague who doesn't know us?

The purpose of the questions just listed is to lead the customer toward the testimonials we would like to capture. It's okay to ask about specific areas of your value like this. When I interview my clients' customers, I want to know about the impact on the customers' lives and work. How, specifically, do my clients help in the areas of time, money, and elsewhere? If you feel you can use some testimonials in a specific area, say, for example, shipping times, you can ask about that: "How do you feel about our shipping times? And how does that help you when we deliver on time?"

Like that. Ask and they shall answer.

Your happy customers will not hesitate to tell you what's on their minds.

Quantify and Emotionalize

As you talk to your customers, aim to quantify and emotionalize the feedback they give you. Quantify it like this:

> For example, if a customer talks about you saving time, ask, "How *much* time, would you guess?"
>
> If a customer says you save them money, ask, "Give me an idea, how *much* money, do you think?"
>
> If a customer says you're one of their best suppliers, quantify that too:
>
> "How many suppliers do you work with in total?"

Let's say the customer says, "20."

You say: "And if you stacked them up from best to worst, and ranked them on the kinds of things we're talking about here—saving you time, being reliable, and delivering on time—where would you rank us in the 20?" They will most likely say toward the very top.

Also work on getting to the emotion these numbers generate.

Customer: "You save me time."

You: "How much time?"

Customer: "I'd guess 20 percent."

You: "Wow! 20 percent in one day a week or 52 days a year?! Am I right on that?"

Customer: "*At least* that much." (Common response: *at least* that much.)

You: "That's amazing! Thank you so much for this compliment. Have you ever thought about it this way before?"

Customer: "I guess not."

You: "And how do you feel about that now that you've said it that way?"

Feel. That's the request for emotion.

Customer: "That's amazing. It's wonderful. I feel like I absolutely made the right choice, and I'd tell anyone they would, too."

There it is.

The customer said that working with you is amazing and wonderful, and that he *absolutely* made the right choice. And they'd tell anybody who asks!

There's the power of having these kinds of conversations with your customers.

This kind of feedback does not walk in the door.

You have to go get it.

Obtain Permission to Use These Comments

Toward the end of your time for the interview, close with the following statement and request:

I want to thank you so much for your time. I really appreciate you doing this, and I'm grateful for your comments and feedback. Is it okay with you if we use some of your comments in our materials?

This is your request for permission to share their testimonials.

Nearly everybody will agree.

And why wouldn't they?

They've just been glowing about you for 10 minutes. They love you. Of course they don't mind if you use their comments.

Most people say, "Of course you can!" Or "Anything you need!" Because people *appreciate the opportunity to help you!*

You help them a great deal, every day, and now they're happy to help you.

The only people who won't grant permission are those who work at very large companies with legal and public relations departments. They will likely decline because they are not allowed to speak about the company in the public domain. If this happens to you, just take a step back and ask them if you can use their first name and company name with their comments. If they are still not comfortable, take another step back: "What if I use only your general job title and describe the company: 'Purchasing Manager at a Fortune 500 technology manufacturer'—would that be okay with you?" At this point, nearly all of these folks will agree.

A Note on Language

We will dig into language in depth in the next part of the book, but I wanted to make an important point here about your language for getting these powerful testimonials.

Talk to the customer as though you're having a drink together.

If you don't drink, imagine you're two friends having a cup of coffee together.

Be conversational.

Be comfortable.

Ask questions in easy, breezy language. Make your requests easy to agree to.

Not "give me testimonials," but "what are some of your favorite things about working with us?" People get stressed out with the word "testimonials." They clam up. They don't know what to say. But ask them to talk about what they like best about working with you, and *this answer* they know. They can talk about it all day. They think about it every time the competition calls. They *know* what they like, and they're happy to tell us.

Not "May I put your testimonials on my website?" but "Is it okay with you if I use some of your comments in my materials?" The latter request is not scary. It's comfortable. Elegant, even.

Think about the impact of your language on the person you are talking to.

Have a lightness to your questions.

And be sure of yourself.

If you're anxious and uncomfortable, it will show in your demeanor and your language, your customer will be able to tell, and you will probably have a choppy, awkward conversation.

You've experienced this too: you can *tell* when the other person is nervous. It comes across in their conversation.

If you're comfortable, relaxed, and enjoying yourself, it will also show, and you'll have a pleasant, enjoyable exchange.

There's nothing to be nervous about here. Remember, your customers are happy, and they will be happy to tell you what they love about working with you. Many of them will feel as though you are doing *them* the favor!

Enjoy your conversation. This is fun!

Use Silence

There's an important component to doing these interviews that's not obvious from the coaching so far.

We need to use silence to our advantage, and the customer's advantage, to give them an opportunity to think about the answers to our questions.

Don't fill the silence with uncomfortable chatter.

Ask a question and wait for the customer to answer it.

You have been preparing to ask these questions for a while, but the customer has not been thinking about them.

You may have a script of questions in front of you, but the customer does not have her answers written out. Let her think!

Now, if she is obviously struggling, and doesn't know the answer, don't leave her hanging. Help her.

More on silence in Chapter 23.

The Script! (Or, What to Ask Your Customers during Your Testimonial Interviews)

Is it okay with you if I record the call?
What are some of your favorite things about working with us?

Follow up:

Why?
How?
In what way?
Tell me more about that . . .
Why did you say that?

Pivot to the value:

How does that help you?
What gets better for you when we do this?
How does your job (or life) get easier when we do this?

Listen actively:

Wow!
No kidding?
Really?
That's pretty amazing, isn't it?

Ask specific questions:

Does working with us save you time?
Does working with us save you money?
Does working with us *make* you money?

How would you describe working with us to a colleague?

Quantify:

How *much* time would you guess we save you?

How *much* money do you think you make as a result of us doing what we do?

Emotionalize:

How do you feel about that?

How does that make you feel?

Ask for permission:

Thank you *so* much for this wonderful feedback. I appreciate it so much. Is it okay with you if we use some of your comments in our materials?

19

Transcript of Actual Customer Interviews

In my last book, *The Revenue Growth Habit,* I laid out what a sample conversation would sound like.

For this book, I got permission from a client to use transcripts from an actual conversation that I did with his customer. In this chapter, I give you excerpts from this customer interview. (Since my client granted permission, I will identify him, but I will protect his customer's privacy and not reveal her real name or the company name.)

The Customer

This customer is a product manager for a large packaging distributor.

Let's call her Jill.

Jill buys from my client, Artistic Carton, which makes cartons (but not corrugated boxes) for retailers—think the gift boxes you get when you buy clothing at the mall—and industrial applications like the carton that goes around an air filter. They print the cartons, stamp them, die-cut them, and pretty much everything else. Artistic Carton is one of several hundred companies in North America that makes these kinds of cartons, but one of just five that owns its own paper mill. This means the other carton companies must buy their paper from suppliers, but Artistic is one of just five "integrated" companies that can make its own paper.

The owner of Artistic Carton, and my client, is Pete Traeger. I am working with him and all of his customer-facing staff.

Reminder: This is a direct transcript of the call between me and the customer, Jill, about Pete's company, Artistic Carton. *My comments are in italics.*

Alex   What do you like best about working with them? What are some of your favorite things?

Jill   Honestly, Pete: he's one of the nicest guys, vendors, that I work with. I know he's honest or I think he's honest. Nothing is a game. He'll tell it, tell me like it is. Respectful. He gets the information back to me when he says or prior to that, so he's really responsive. He's just down to earth. I don't know, what we do should not be hard and he doesn't make it hard. So I appreciate that.

Here are our threads:

1. *Pete is one of the nicest people I work with.*
2. *They're honest.*
3. *He's really responsive.*
4. *He's down to earth.*
5. *He doesn't make it hard. (It's easy to work with Artistic.)*

I could pick any of these and dive into a deeper discussion, but I am interested in the final item, so I pull that thread.

Alex   You said, "What we do shouldn't be hard and he doesn't make it hard." Talk about that. Why is that? Can you tell me about that one?

Jill   I just work with some other vendors that . . . asking them for dimensions is difficult. Asking them for costs; it's just a game. With Pete, it's not a game. I ask him, "Can you do this? Tell me how it works," and he's like, "Well, we can do everything." Or, he might say, "Well, this is going to get really expensive or we could do it this way." So I guess, to me, he's just really transparent and upfront. He follows through. Again, these are all things that you would expect, but as a customer, sometimes it's shocking.

I even joked with him when he called and asked me for this interview that you're calling for. I was like, "Pete, the fact that you're even having a consultant, and this is your thought process, already tells you that, to me, you don't have a problem. You're the least of my vendors that should be hiring consultants."

Does it sound like it's easy to work with the competition? Does it sound like working with other companies is a pleasure for her? No, it sounds rather terrible. She says it's shocking *when people do things that are expected and straightforward.*

She also makes it a point to say that she is impressed that Artistic is even doing this interview. I didn't ask her about it; she volunteered it. That's an important point. That piece came at the end of this answer. If I had jumped in to ask my next question, she never would have said it. But I stayed quiet and let her keep talking. Let silence work its magic for you.

Now, I want to know how Artistic stacks up against other providers.

Alex   How many vendors do you work with, Jill?

Jill   Oh Lord, over 50.

Alex   So you deal with 50 suppliers, and if you were to rank them from best to worst on the kinds of things we're talking about now, which is responsiveness, getting answers, honesty, doing what he says he's going to do, being upfront; all these things you're telling me about, where would you rank Artistic and Pete on that list?

Jill   Oh, in the top five.

Alex   Top five?

Jill   Yeah, and I'm not even sure who, if anyone would be above him, but . . . yeah. I don't dread talking to Pete. There are other vendors that I honestly dread even reaching out to them.

She dreads talking to some of her vendors!

Alex   What percentage do you dread of the 50?

Jill   That's just my own reflection. I would say probably a third of them.

Alex   It's not your fault. It's their fault. A third?!

Jill   Yeah, probably a third.

Alex   Wow. Of course, they're probably the ones you have to talk to the most.

Jill   Exactly.

She dreads talking to 17 of her 50 suppliers! Dreads. That's an enormously powerful statement.

Alex   How do you guys interact?

Jill   I think he has come in twice for formal meetings. But otherwise,
         I usually email him and he usually calls me.

Alex   Are you okay talking on the phone with suppliers?

Jill   Yes, with Pete. But with a lot of them I would rather email, because
         I don't trust them. I want a documentation that's written.

Alex   Wow, really? But it's not that way with Pete?

Jill   No, because again, he's just pleasant. We can have a conversation.
         I know that he's going to do what we're talking about. If anything,
         if he tells me he can get it out by Thursday and it's Wednesday and
         he can't do it until Friday, I get three emails apologizing that he's not
         going to get it until Friday. You know what I mean?
         Customers say that to me a lot: they do what they say they're going to do.
         I always thought that if you're in business, you have to do what you say you're
         going to do. But this is not true. It's a rare commodity. Most of the competition
         is not reliable. You need to know this. The competition is not as good as you,
         and the customer knows it. Just listen to her!
         Now I am going to pivot to the value.

Alex   Yeah. How does it help you when he does these things? When he's
         consistent and on time and responsive and all of these things. Does
         what he says, how does it help, Jill?

Jill   It makes my job a heck of a lot easier. I am confident in telling my
         managers and going upstream and I'm confident that what he's
         telling me will happen. That what I'm saying is, in fact, the truth, and
         that he's going to deliver on it. It's interesting because Pete has taught
         me about the manufacturing process and what he does, and I've used
         that and now I can tell that other manufacturers are giving me a line!
         Here's what she's saying: Pete won't make me look like an idiot with my
         colleagues. I can trust what he is telling me. Not only that, he has helped me
         figure out when my other vendors aren't being honest with me. What a
         tremendous relationship!

Alex   So does working with Artistic make your job easier?

Jill   It makes my job easier, and it makes me want to do more business
         with them.
         Whoa!
         Then we talked some more about what makes her want to do more business
         with them. We talked some more about responsiveness, dependability, and

trust. Then I changed gears, and we talked about whether working with Artistic saves her time.

Alex   Does working with Pete and Artistic save you time, say, as compared to doing it with a more average one of your 50?

Jill   Sure, because there's less back and forth. The product is the same, but in the sense that, on the rare occasion if we do have a quality issue, there isn't the back and forth and the squabbling. Pete is just like, "Oh, let us know what it is and we'll take care of it." So yeah, in that sense, it saves me time.

Now, we quantify.

Alex   How much time do you think? If you had to do it with a more middle-of-the-pack kind of a supplier, how much longer do you think it would take, or how much faster? How much time does it save with Pete?

Jill   Twenty to 30 percent.

Alex   Really?

Jill   Yeah.

Alex   Wow. That's a big number.

What an amazing compliment. What an incredibly powerful testimonial. Working with Artistic Carton saves "20 to 30 percent" of her time. What can Pete possibly say about Artistic that's better than this?!

Jill   Pete's a businessman. He understands. He sees the bigger picture. You can tell that either that's his professional development or just how he is as a person. With other people it's kind of like, I have other contacts who focus on the nickels and dimes. Granted, Pete also owns the company so it's up to him. He can make those decisions. He's in power to do so, so maybe that's part of the comparison too, that these other mid-tier manufacturers, the people that I'm dealing with, don't own the company. But they get focused on the small stuff, you know, and they don't see the forest through the trees. I don't slice hairs with Pete. He gets it. We make a decision and move on. And I like that too, that I actually work with Pete as the owner.

Alex   Yeah, tell me about that. What does that mean to you?

Jill   I know he's the one that's making the decisions, and if I don't get anything I know he's going to get down to it and figure it out. I got the sense that people that worked for him respected him and they truly enjoyed what they did, or at least they liked working there.

We talked some more and the call ended with me asking for, and receiving, permission for Artistic Carton to use Jill's testimonials.

What Happened

So let's debrief what happened here.

What the Customer Is Talking About

What is the customer talking about?

Products?

There was really not one word about products, was there?

In fact, even after speaking to her for 20 minutes (my calls are bit longer and dive a bit deeper than yours need to), I don't even exactly know which products she buys from Artistic. Nor do I care. Because it doesn't really matter for our purposes here. I know this will be hard for you, because products and services are what *you* talk about with customers. But why didn't Jill talk about the product? Because it's a commodity. She doesn't really care about the details of the cartons. She cares about how easy they are to buy from Artistic. And how nice it is to work with Pete. And that he's honest with her, because many of the others aren't.

What else is she not talking about? No mention of price, is there?

And she does not bring up problems with orders.

So, no product, no problems, no price.

What do you talk about with customers?

Yep: products and price and problems.

I want you to think and talk about your work more like your customers do.

They talk about the value and experience and relationship. That's what her comments center on, isn't it? About the *relationship* she has with Pete and the company. It's about *what it's like to work with them,* not about their products.

The products are commodities, but the relationships are singular.

They can buy the products anywhere.

But they can only get the relationship from *you*. The relationship is singular.

Focus on the relationships.

Your customers do.

The Conversation Itself

What's your take on this conversation?

Does it feel like I'm extracting things from this customer that she doesn't want to share with me?

Am I pulling things from her that she's trying not to share?

Not even close, right?

In fact, if we were old friends meeting for lunch, or a drink, the conversation would sound very much like this.

Nice and easy.

Just two friends having a chat.

This is how you should talk to your customers in these interviews.

Like you are friends. (That's what they feel about you, anyway.)

Like you care about them. (Also true. Right?)

You're just having a chat. Comfortable and easy.

Trust your relationship.

Trust that they're happy.

Trust that you're damn good.

And just a have conversation with your customer.

The Testimonials

This portion of the chapter contains the finished set of testimonials from the conversation in this chapter. I want you to see what the end product looks like. (Some of these comments come from portions of the conversation I did not include in the transcript.)

- Pete is one of the nicest people I have ever worked with. He doesn't play games, he's very responsive, and he's just down to earth.

- I work with other vendors, and asking them for dimensions is difficult. Cost is difficult. It feels like a game. With Pete it's not a game. I just ask him, "Will it work?" and he tells me.

- I really appreciate that Pete is very transparent and upfront.

- Of my 50 vendors, Artistic Carton would be within the top five. I don't really know who would be ahead of them.

- I don't dread talking to Pete, as I do with other vendors. I dread talking to at least a third of them.

- Pete takes the time to hand-deliver samples. Because I don't trust a lot of my vendors, I want things in writing. But with Pete, a phone call is fine. He's just pleasant and you can have a conversation.

- I know he's going to do what we're talking about. I am confident he is telling me the truth.

- Working with Pete makes my job a heck of a lot easier. I'm confident in what he's telling me that it's the truth. He has taught me about the manufacturing process, which helps me deal with other vendors as well.

- Because of the trust and confidence, I want to do more business with him.

- When products and projects come up, I always first wonder if Artistic can do the work and I don't hesitate to reach out.

- It is 20 to 30 percent faster to work with Artistic Carton. With them, there is less back and forth. Pete just says let me know what it is and we'll take care of it.

- I like that I actually work with Pete as the owner. I know he's the one making the decision. I get the sense that people who work for him respect him. They like working there.

- It is advantageous to me that Artistic Carton owns that mill, and that Pete has so much industry knowledge.

That's 13 deep, rich, detailed testimonials from a brief conversation. The total number of testimonials extracted was 22. That's more than one testimonial per minute of talking.

You can do this too.

Exactly like this!

20 | How to Use Testimonials Internally to Change Your Mindset and Your Culture

So, now you have your testimonials.

What will you do with them?

How do you use them?

In Chapter 30, I show you how to sell with them, externally.

In this chapter, I talk about how to use them internally, with your colleagues and staff members, in order to create the mindset shifts discussed in Part II. Here is how to leverage the testimonials you get to turn fear into confidence, meekness into boldness, and pessimism into optimism.

The point of all of this—talking to customers, obtaining testimonials, and having them read and review them regularly—is for you to understand and *believe* how good you are. Because knowing how good you are is key to making the mindset shifts needed. Once you begin to believe how good you are, and you start making some of the key mindset shifts we've discussed, you can start behaving accordingly and taking the simple but systematic actions discussed in the next part of this book.

Who Should See These Testimonials?

The short answer is everybody. There is nobody at your company who would not benefit from this kind of incredibly positive feedback from happy customers. The customer-facing people and those in the office would benefit in amazing ways, and those are who this chapter is about. But what about the folks in the manufacturing plant? Or in the warehouse? Or the good people in the shipping department? Or the people on the receiving dock, or the quality control folks? They would all be amazed to see the extraordinary results of their work. They all *deserve* to see that this is the ultimate outcome of their work.

We Must Marinate in This Positivity

These testimonials need to be shared, presented, shown, and discussed regularly. Once is not enough. Once gets us to "Oh, that's interesting." But we need repeated exposure over extended periods of time to get to "This is what I do, and my customers love us!"

So think about ways to consistently get these testimonials in front of your sales and customer service people, at least.

If You're a Manager, Here Is What to Do

Email them. Email *all* of them, and then email them as they come in. And then go back to the original set and email them one at a time.

If you're doing internal presentations, put them in your slide deck.

Print them and hand them out.

Discuss them in meetings.

Put them on the walls. I have clients who have created "Walls of Love"—their words—where testimonials are printed in a large font, laminated, and placed on the walls throughout the company. Other clients have written them on windows and glass partitions in dry-erase markers. Put them in the areas where people sit so that they have to see them as they come and go.

If you do the interviews and record the calls, share the audio.

Email the audio.

But also *play* the audio.

If You're a Salesperson, Here Is How to Change Your Mindset with These Testimonials

Refer to them daily.

They are your mindset bible.

Print them out and put them on your desk.

You can create a single sheet of key testimonials, front and back, in small print.

Keep the testimonials around in hard copy because if they're digital, they're easy to ignore. Files accumulate on your computer. New files push less urgent ones into the background.

Put them up on the walls of your office or on the partitions around your desk.

Do you spend your days driving? Place a sheet of testimonials in your center console or glove compartment.

Keep a digital note on your smart phone, so you can refer to it.

If you record the audio, listen to it on a regular basis.

Let it sink in.

Listen to it before you go to sleep at night so that it's the last thing you feed your mind.

Listen to them, or read them, before sales meetings.

I need you to believe that the customer is lucky to have you there. You could be anywhere, but you are *there* with *that* customer, and how lucky are *they?!*

Marinate in the positivity of your happy customers, so that you *know* how good you are and then behave accordingly.

That's what's next: behaving accordingly.

Here come the sales-growing actions!

PART IV

From Mindset to Technique: Powerful Sales Growth Actions

21

About These Communications

Now that you know the mindsets that lead to fast sales growth and how to quickly attain them, let's talk about the actions. Part IV covers what to do to grow sales. If you've been reading the book from the beginning, this is the stuff you've been waiting for. But if you skipped ahead to this part, I do think these actions will make total sense to you, but it will be more difficult for you to implement them repeatedly and systematically (more on these two words shortly) unless you've worked through the earlier parts on the right outlook and how to attain it.

They Are All Communications

Every action described in Part IV is just a communication with a customer and prospect.

Want to grow sales?

Communicate more with people who can pay you.

The more we communicate with customers and prospects, the more they buy.

The less we communicate, the less they buy.

It never works the other way. You can never communicate less and sell more. But every time you communicate more with your market, they will buy more. Why is this? Because you are *reminding* them to buy from you and you are also *educating* them about *what* they can buy from you.

This entire system is built around communicating more with people who can pay you.

That's it.

I Know You Know This

Some of the chapters to come are quite brief.

I know you know about these techniques already.

I know you know you should ask for referrals and also let customers know about what else they can buy from you.

Of course you know.

You earn a living selling.

The question is, are you *doing* these proactive activities enough? Or, perhaps a better question is, do you have a few seconds per day to do more of them to sell more, help your customers more, and take home more money?

If you can give me one minute per day, you can implement a handful of these communications every day. That's 20 proactive communications per week, 80 per month, and nearly 1,000 new proactive efforts per year. How can your sales *possibly* not grow when your proactive communications are exponentially increased like this?

I know you know.

But here, today, in this section, we talk about *doing* what you know!

Don't Overcomplicate It

At a recent speech with 100 or so business owners in attendance, during the portion of my session on the importance of being present with customers and showing them you care, one owner raised his hand and stated (he didn't ask, he stated): "People have different strengths and weaknesses and personality profiles, so this is not for everybody."

My answer was that he was overcomplicating it.

It's simpler than that.

Just let people know what else they can buy from you.

Just ask for the business.

What is your customer buying elsewhere that you can help with?

You can do this whatever your personality profile.

You can do this whatever your strengths and weaknesses.

I'll give you the questions. All you have to do is ask them.

If you think you may not remember what to say, print them, tape them to your monitor, and simply read them.

That's all you have to do. Read them.

The communications detailed in this part of the book are fast, easy ways to show your customers you care about them and you would like to do more with them. People appreciate this. They value this. And here's a major key: your competition is *not* communicating in this way.

After I explained this, another business owner raised his hand and asked, "What if the customer's psychology doesn't allow for this?"

I responded: "What do you think you're doing here? What's happening right now?"

Him: Silence.

Me: Staring.

Him: "Complicating it?"

Me: "Yes, sir."

Him: "It's easier than that, isn't it?"

Me: "Yes, sir."

Him: "Right."

Me: "My work here is done."

Use "Easy" Language

The same language rules apply for the sales growth actions described here as in Chapter 18, where we discussed how to get testimonials:

- You use comfortable language, like you're talking with a friend, not a buyer.

- If you don't feel pressure, the customer won't feel pressure. But if you are feeling the pressure, it will come through in what you say. Speak easy.

Laugh. Enjoy yourself. If this person doesn't buy, there are a thousand others.

- Use easy-breezy language. Don't use stressful words like "testimonial" and "referral." Instead say, "What do you like best?" and "Who do you know?"
    - Not "Will you give me a testimonial?" but "Do you have a few minutes to give me some feedback about how we're doing for you?"
    - Not "May I put your testimonials on my website?" but "Is it okay with you if we use some of your comments in our materials?"
    - Not "Let's close this deal" but "How many would you like?"
    - Not "What happened to that quote?" but "Where are you at on that quote we discussed?

Use language that makes it easy for the customer to say yes.

Mostly, ask questions. Be curious and helpful.

As you make your plan, ask yourself, "How can I make this easier for the customer to say yes to?" Then simplify it. Take the pressure out of it.

Or, to make your life really easy, just read the language of the script in the pages that follow.

Print out the script, place it in front of you, and read it—but with a smile. Practice this. "Did you know we also sell . . . ?"

Having a plan will help you feel comfortable and in control. You should know *what* you're doing each day and the language you will use.

Do You Have a Few Seconds?

If you have a few seconds during your day, you can do this work.

The did you know question (see Chapter 27) takes three seconds to ask.

The pivot to the sale (Chapter 26) takes two seconds.

The reverse did you know question (Chapter 28) takes three seconds. You *have* the time.

And here's the best thing: you don't even have to pick up the phone to do most of these actions. You can just ask them in existing phone calls.

So, please don't tell me you're too busy.

Even if you give me 10 of these actions each day, it's still less than one minute of work altogether.

You have the time.

Now it's time to do the work.

It Doesn't Take Money to Make Money

None of these actions cost any money. There is nothing to pay for here. I'm not asking you to buy advertising, or get on airplanes, or buy gifts for customers.

In fact, the statement that "it takes money to make money" is believed and cited by many, but it's totally untrue, and even asinine for our purposes. It doesn't take money to make money. It takes a minimum amount of personal effort. It takes a little elbow grease.

It takes some attention, paid by you to your customers and prospects.

So, pay them the attention.

It's better than paying the money.

What If My Day Is Totally Reactive?

A woman came up to me after a workshop recently, and asked this excellent question: "How do I do these actions if my day is totally reactive? I spend my days dealing with incoming call after incoming call."

A smart, insightful question.

Here's the answer: most of these actions are designed to be integrated into your existing day.

That is, *infuse these proactive actions, most of which require just a few seconds each, into your otherwise reactive day.*

You can ask many of the questions—including the did you know question and reverse did you know question—in five seconds or less during already planned phone calls.

You can ask for referrals during existing calls.

You can even follow up on quotes and proposals during current conversations.

Look for places to inject these actions throughout your day.

That's the key.

Keep the actions in front of you and I'll give you the planning tools to do so in this part of the book.

Then, simply do the work throughout your day.

Repeatedly and Systematically

Although the actions are fast, the magic is in the repetition and the systems.

One did you know question is not enough.

One referral request isn't, either.

It takes sustained multiple efforts.

Why not ask everybody you talk to during the day a did you know question?

Why not ask for two referrals per day, which is 10 weekly, 40 monthly, and 480 annually. If you close just 20 percent of them—and you should close at least that many referrals—you're looking at nearly 100 new customers. That's a big deal.

With quantity, we turn snowflakes into blizzards. That is, small actions add up to big results, just as in the example of referrals leading to new customers. But without quantity, we just have a snowflake or two, which quickly melt and disappear. On their own, these actions are better than nothing. But in groups, in bunches, they've added up to 10 to 20 percent growth annually for my clients.

Quantity trumps quality in sales growth. We need a high quantity of these communications, but not necessarily perfect communications. This is a hard concept for many people. The product or service needs to be close to perfect. The communications do not. They merely need to be helpful. So plan—and do!—as large a quantity of these communications as you can.

And the new revenue will take care of itself.

It's Impossible to Overcommunicate

Every communication action presented in this part of the book adds value to your customers and prospects.

It's impossible to overcommunicate.

You're not selling or pitching or annoying.

You're not sending promotions or sales or discounts.

You're adding value.

You are alerting your customers and prospects to additional products they can buy.

You are trying to help them more.

You are teaching them.

You are trying to get their products or services to them faster.

And here's another reason that it's impossible to overcommunicate: people forget!

Just because you tell somebody something doesn't mean they know it.

That's why people so frequently say, "I didn't know you did that." You might have told them about it two weeks ago, but today, they do not remember.

We remember everything we say and communicate, because we worry about overdoing it.

But we should stop this worrying.

It costs us a lot of money.

The customer doesn't remember.

In fact, your communication may never register at all. They may *hear* it, but not *know* it.

This is why we must keep communicating with them, frequently and systematically.

And this is why it's impossible to overcommunicate.

If you're communicating the Selling Boldly actions detailed in this part of the book, you can't overdo it.

So stop worrying about it.

Simple, But Not Easy

None of these actions are difficult.

They are not complicated.

They are, in fact, quite simple.

Most of them you can just read from a script, which I provide.

You can also download the scripts from my website at www.goldfayn .com.

The work is simple and straightforward.

But it's not necessarily easy to implement systematically.

If it was, everybody would be doing it!

The questions are simple, but it's not always easy to (1) remember to ask them, (2) repeat this throughout the day, (3) track the results, and (4) stay accountable to this all-important process through your otherwise reactive day.

As you read through these actions, they will seem quite easy.

You will think to yourself that you already know these things.

And you will be correct.

But ask yourself, how many of them are you doing regularly and systematically, proactively?

If you are like most salespeople, the answer will be not many, if any.

This work is simple, but not necessarily easy to do the right way.

And the sales growth we are looking for comes from the doing.

We need to *do*.

Designed to Set You Apart

Everything that follows has been built to put you in front of your customers and prospects in ways that the competition is not.

I want you to stand out.

I want you to be present.

I want you to show people you care.

Before the Internet, the telephone was all we had, so everybody called. There weren't other choices. These days, almost nobody calls (see Chapter 25 for more on the power of making proactive calls). So, if you pick up the phone today to call a customer with nothing urgent, you may be the only one doing so.

When you follow up on a quote or proposal, you should know that most of the competition is not doing this.

When you tell your customers about what else they can buy, know that you are setting yourself apart from the competition, which sits and waits for the customer to call *them*.

Let them wait.

We'll go to the customer.

We'll be the only ones.

Quick Wins

These actions result in quick wins, which are necessary to turn new behaviors into habits.

For example: 20 percent of all did you know questions close. Ask five did you know questions on your first day of doing this work, and you should be able to add one new line item, one new additional sale, that you didn't have the day before.

Similarly, 20 to 30 percent of quote follow-ups done in the way that I teach you in Chapter 29 result in that outstanding quote closing.

Follow up on five quotes today, and you should close at least one.

This work leads to quick wins.

So you can see this works.

So you can get excited.

So you start wanting to do more of it.

It's its own righteous circle.

Your new proactive effort will lead to fast successes and fairly immediate results.

Give Customers and Prospects a Backscratcher

If you communicate with customers or prospects sporadically, or rarely, you must time your communications to their needs.

You have to hope to connect with them with precisely the product or service they need, at the exact time that they need it.

This is very difficult to do.

You need to hope they have the precise itch that you are offering to scratch, at the moment you are offering it. All of this coming together perfectly is highly unlikely, which is why selling this way is extremely challenging, with a very high (and understandable) burnout rate.

Now, if you communicate *regularly* and *systematically*—as in, all the time—you don't have to worry about timing your offer to scratch to the customer's itch.

With this approach—the one we introduce in this part of the book—you are placing a backscratcher on your customer's desk. The backscratcher has your name on it.

The customer sees and hears your name all the time in conjunction with extremely helpful information.

They know the backscratcher is there.

And when they get an itch, they pick up the backscratcher, and they scratch.

They pick up the phone, and they call you with their need.

But this only works if you are in front of them regularly and consistently.

That's the work.

That's what we talk about in the ensuing chapters.

In baseball, they call this the payoff pitch.

Here, let's call these the money chapters.

In the pages ahead, I teach you exactly how to help your customers more, how to create more customers, and how to take more money home to your family, which they so richly deserve.

22

Focus on What You Can Control

Sports Are Like Sales

During interviews, professional athletes often talk about focusing on what they can control. You might hear them say, "I can't worry about things other people are doing." Or, "I just focus on myself, put in the work, and the results will take care of themselves."

Many professional athletes repeat this because their coaches and sports psychologists drill it into their minds.

In baseball, batters focus on their swing mechanics. Can they move their hands through the strike zone faster? Are their hips positioned correctly? Should they choke up on the bat? Are they stepping with their front foot the right way?

What the batter *cannot* control, however, is where the ball will go. Whether it flies into a gap on the field for a hit, or directly at a defender for an out, the outcome is beyond the player's control, so he tries to not worry about it.

In golf, it's the same process: focus on your swing. Consistency is key, the same swing every time. A nice, smooth motion. Keep the head as still

163

as possible. (If this sounds like I don't golf, it's because I don't! But I've heard friends and clients talking about it.)

Athletes focus on their diet, because they can control it. But whether the coach plays them or not is outside of their purview. They focus on getting enough rest and plenty of sleep, because that's up to them. But they can't control whether they will start the next game or whether they will be traded, so they will tell you they try not to concern themselves about it.

Of course, they are not always successful, and that is when they start running into problems. If a baseball player is using proper swing mechanics but keeps getting outs because the ball is not flying to open spots on the field, he might get down or upset. Then he'll lose focus on his swing mechanics and *they* will suffer. The one process within his control will suffer when he shifts his focus to areas he cannot control.

The hits will come. He simply needs to keep swinging the right way.

Focus on What You Can Control in Sales Too

Sales is the same way.

We must focus on what we can control.

We are in charge of our communications. We can control the amount of proactive effort we put into our sales, and we can choose to persevere and try again. These things are up to us. We can also determine the *kinds* of effort we put forth. Are we communicating personally, on the phone or face to face? Or are we reverting to sending emails, which are far less personal and have much less impact?

Measure those things you can control.

And don't focus on—or measure—whether the customer buys or not. That's not up to us. We can only affect our part of this equation—the work that leads the customer to decide whether working with us (or working with us more) is in his or her best interest. We can ask a series of did you know questions, ask for the sale, and then follow up on our quote or proposal. We can do our bit, but we cannot do the buying for the customer. So don't worry about that part.

Your job is to take your swings. The hits (sales) will come.

That's because we cannot control if the customer decides to go with a competitor because their price is slightly lower. Or, perhaps, the customer's budget dries up. Or maybe his boss has a long-standing relationship with another vendor, so they go with that company. You can't control these things, so don't worry about them.

Just take your swings. Take your cuts, as they say in baseball.

We want practiced, effective, efficient, *proactive* swings.

Of course, *our* swings are communications.

Communicate personally.

Focus on your value.

Tell the customer all the ways that you can help her.

Ask key questions, like what are they buying elsewhere that you can help them with.

Ask questions that pivot to the sale.

Show them you are interested in them.

Show them you won't let them down.

Show them you are reliable.

Show them you care.

Take your swings.

The hits will come.

The sales will come.

You do what you do.

The right customers—the good ones, the ones you want—will see your value.

Focus on your mechanics.

Take your swings.

And the sales will come.

23 | Silence Is Money

Want to know the most underutilized technique in sales?

Silence.

That's right.

Not talking is a rare commodity in the sales profession.

In fact, salespeople are constantly talking at your customers.

At first I was going to include this material in the previous chapter, with the other key elements of implementing these communications. But then I decided that silence is so important and so undervalued that it needs to be considered separately, in its own chapter.

Here's What I Mean by Silence

Silence is:

Asking for a referral and waiting for the answer.

Asking for a testimonial and waiting until the customer answers.

Asking for the business and not speaking until the customer responds.

Silence means not filling the pauses with your nervous chatter.
Too much *money* is lost when you fill the pauses with nervous chatter.

Why We Are Not Silent

Why do we talk into the silences?
    Because we are nervous.
    Because are not confident, or bold, or sure of our value.
    But now you are, right?
    Now you know how good you are.
    Because you see how valuable you are to your customers.
    We don't "do" silence because we think the customer is unhappy, or uncomfortable, when he is quiet. In actuality, he is merely thinking, and when we jump into that pause, we interrupt his decision-making.
    Let your customer think and consider your question.
    Let them answer.
    Then, you go.

How to Be Silent

Here are two ways to use silence to your advantage.

Ask One of the Questions in the Chapters That Follow and Then WAIT

Here is how to be silent: Ask one of our questions—like the did you know question or the reverse did you know question or a closing question—and then stop. And wait.
    If you are together with the customer, just look at them, and blink. Breathe. Be confident and comfortable.
    Count to 100 if you must.
    Sing a song in your head.

(When my kids were younger, I'd have them sing their ABCs while they washed their hands with soap. Otherwise, they'd just touch the water with their fingertips and then turn off the water.)

Do what you have to do to not talk first!

During Conversation

The other powerful use of silence is within a conversation, during the back and forth.

When the other person finishes up what they're saying, *don't* start talking right away. Wait two beats. If they don't say anything else, then you start.

You will find that the other person may jump back into that silence with something you wouldn't have even known to ask about.

Many times during my testimonial calls, there are long pauses because I take notes while the other person speaks. And because they talk faster than I can type, I am frequently catching up with what they are saying. So, as I type, I simply say, "Catching up," and the other person almost always says, "No problem" or "Take your time." But then, in approximately *half* of these pauses—which is multiple times per phone call!—the customer jumps back into the silence and volunteers information I would have had no idea to ask about. Something like: "And then there was the time he got in his car and drove the part over here. How amazing is that?!" There's no way I could have inquired about this if the customer did not bring it up.

It works the same in conversation.

The customer might say, "Well, we've got that project at the school that you know about already."

You: One-thousand-one, one-thousand-two . . .

Customer: "But we ran into a problem that you might be able to help us with . . ."

That's how this works.

Don't be the person who starts talking before the customer finishes their sentence.

You will find many people communicate this way. They can't *wait* to tell you their piece.

That's insecurity and discomfort coming through in their portion of the conversation.

I find this with about one-third of the people I talk to.

That's okay.

I still pause before taking my turn in the conversation.

And they think of additional things to say during the silences that are often of high value to me.

Use silence to help the other person think of new things to share with you.

Silence is rare.

Silence is a sign of confidence.

Silence is a feature of an advanced and outstanding salesperson.

Use silence.

Because silence is money.

24 | Don't Forget about the Prospects

Because most salespeople work reactively, we spend our days dealing with calls from customers.

Some call this order-taking.

Some call it gathering.

Some call it serving the customer.

All of these are correct. But when you sell this way—and most people do—you're limiting yourself almost entirely to interactions with customers.

You sell to people who are already buying from you.

The *prospects* aren't calling with problems or urgent orders.

By definition, only customers are making those calls.

And that's who we talk to all day.

When I ask salespeople at my clients' companies what percent of their communications are with prospects, the answers almost always come in at under 10 percent.

So: Yes, it's easy to sell more to existing customers.

They *want* to buy more from you.

But: you have many prospects out there who are currently doing business with your competition. These people would be so much better off with you.

You would help them more than the competition is.

You would be timelier with your delivery.

You would be more available when they call.

You would save them more time than the competition currently does because of how well and how quickly you work.

Prospects would get far more value from you than they do from the competition.

Why Prospects Are Sales Growth Gold

Whether you manufacture or distribute products, or deliver services, prospects are revenue gold.

Why?

Because they buy for the first time only once. After this, they become a repeat customer.

And that's where you make your living, on repeat business.

One of my clients—an owner of a large pipe and valve distributor—says that my customers eat a pizza from him and then they need more pizza because they get hungry again. Your customers use your products or services and then they need some more.

Prospects are incredibly valuable because they are only one order away from being a repeat customer.

So don't forget about the prospects.

Make it a part of your day to spend some time talking with people who are not current customers.

Use the "Proactive Call Planner" to make a concrete list of prospects you can communicate with. Download your free copy at Goldfayn.com.

PROACTIVE CALL PLANNER

Date Range:

What To Say On These Calls
- Just checking in.
- I was just thinking about you.
- How have you been?
- How's your family?
- What are you working on that I can help with?

Top Customers Who Can Buy More (And WHAT To Offer Them)	Customers I Haven't Talked To In Six Months Or More	Customer Who Used To Buy, But Stopped	Good Customers Who Just Received An Order (Follow-up)

Prospects I Once Talked To (3+ Months) But They Never Bought	Prospects I Know Are Buying Elsewhere Now	Prospects I've Never Talked To, But Want To Make Contact With	Prospects I'm Actively Speaking With, But Have Not Yet Bought

ALEX • GOLDFAYN

The bottom half of the planner has four different kinds of prospects you can talk to. There is more about these prospects in the next chapter on using the phone.

Don't forget about the prospects.

They deserve your great value too.

And you deserve the significant new revenue that comes from them.

PROACTIVE CALL PLANNER

Date Range:

What To Say On These Calls

➤ Just checking in.
➤ I was just thinking about you.
➤ How have you been?
➤ How's your family?
➤ What are you working on that I can help with?

Top Customers Who Can Buy More (And WHAT To Offer Them)	Customers I Haven't Talked To In Six Months Or More	Customers Who Used To Buy, But Stopped	Good Customers Who Just Received An Order (Follow-up)

Prospects I Once Talked To (3+ Months) But They Never Bought	Prospects I Know Are Buying Elsewhere Now	Prospects I've Never Talked To, But Want To Make Contact With	Prospects I'm Actively Speaking With, But Have Not Yet Bought

ALEX • GOLDFAYN

25 | Use the Phone Proactively

Even though our job as salespeople is to talk to humans and help them, we avoid the telephone.

We don't call because we assume the customer is on the phone constantly, being called by everybody. This is not true. Everybody else is *also* avoiding the telephone.

We don't call because we assume we will annoy the customer. This is not true. Most of your customers will be happy to hear from you.

We don't call because we assume the customer will call us if they need us. This is not true. They are busy, so they call only when it's urgent. Like us, they call only when it's reactive for *them*. They do not call proactively. They will simply keep buying things from your competition that *you* could help them with. And they will assume you are not interested, since you are not calling.

It's *our* job to call our customers proactively.

But we do not call, because we are afraid.

We are afraid of being rejected—the top fear for salespeople. We are afraid of making the customer angry. We are afraid of being yelled at. We are afraid, ultimately, of losing the customer.

If I call, the customer will get so mad, she will dump me for the competition.

As covered in depth in Part I of this book, this is an automatic reaction. It usually happens unconsciously.

Because they are so ingrained in us, we are usually not even aware of these fears that keep us from using the phone.

But now you should be aware.

Use the "Proactive Call Planner" in this chapter to lay out the people you will dial up and transfer them to your "One-Page Sales Planner."

And make the calls.

You'll find, like nearly all of my clients do, that it's nice to have a conversation with your customers and prospects when *they don't need anything from you urgently.*

And your customers will also enjoy the interaction.

You will be the only one calling them like this, and it will set you above the competition.

Four Hours a Week

Several years ago I researched how much time outside and inside salespeople spend on the phone.

The goal was to determine the hours spent actively engaged in speaking to customers and prospects on the phone.

What I found did more than surprise me.

It stunned me.

It staggered me.

On average, salespeople spend four hours a week on the phone.

Four!

The best salespeople spend around six hours a week.

The worst ones spend an hour or two weekly.

This begs the question: there are 40 work hours in a week. The job is to talk to people to help them buy from you. The average salesperson spends four hours a week doing this on the phone. What are they doing the other 36 hours?

Here are the top three answers I get:

Email.

Research.

Driving. (*Does the phone work in the car?!*)

The truth is, we avoid the phone.

We'd rather check our fantasy team scores than call customers and prospects.

My clients see their phone time increase from 4 hours a week to 8 to 10 hours. Most clients see a doubling of phone hours, at a minimum. Some triple their phone hours. Ironically, however, you don't increase phone time by asking your salespeople for more hours on the phone. A different approach is needed. More on this a bit later in this chapter.

Telephone Scenes

Here are three powerful stories about the telephone.

"She was so happy to hear from me."

I was interviewing a salesperson for one of my clients, and he brought up a customer of his who he was having some trouble getting on the same page with. He felt like they weren't connecting with each other. She was impatient with him and he wasn't sure why.

He asked me what he should do.

I said, "Call her."

He said "Okay, and . . . "

Me	"And talk to her."
Him	"About what?"
Me	"About how she's doing."
Him	"Really?"
Me	"Yes. She will appreciate it."
Him	"Really?"
Me	"Yes. You'll have a nice conversation."

He was dubious. But he went and did it.

I didn't know this until I was doing this client's live full-day workshop (which is one of the major components of my client projects), and this salesperson raised his hand to tell the story.

"Alex, I just want to tell this story to the group. Alex told me to call this customer, who I wasn't connecting well with. And I did it."

He had my attention.

"She picked up the phone, and I told her it was me, Andy, calling."

Customer	"Hi, what do you need?"
Andy	"Nothing. How are you doing?"
Customer	"Fine. What do you want?"
Andy	"Nothing. Just checking in. I was thinking about you and wanted to reach out."
Customer	"Okay. What's wrong?"
Andy	"Nothing's wrong. I don't need anything. I'm just saying hello. How have you been?"
Customer, stunned	"Really?"
Andy	"Really. How's your family?"
Customer	"Nobody asks me that. Nobody calls me like this."
Andy	"I know. That's why I wanted to."
Customer	"Wow, that's nice."

They had a lovely conversation, he relayed. He never brought up business or products or services.

But guess what?

Two weeks later, she called him and gave him quite a bit more business. She nearly doubled the total business they were doing together.

I asked Andy if he thought she would have called him like this if he didn't make his incredibly high-impact call.

His answer: "No chance. She wouldn't have even thought of me. She only gave us this work because I was in front of her. Because we talked on the phone, and she remembered it."

He gave her the backscratcher with his company's name on it. And when she got the itch, she picked it up and used it. He called her. And then when she needed him, she called him.

That's how it works.

"He needs to call me."

I was with a lumber distributor in South Dakota. (Obviously, I work in very sexy industries!)

They have an executive who is in charge of purchasing *and* sales.

Because lumber is a true commodity, it is essentially traded by people in the business. It is purchased, sometimes altered, and then resold. So at this company the same person did both sides of that work. Let's call him Mark.

He told this story.

Mark had a supplier he had worked with for some time, who made a really terrible mistake on an order.

Mark hammered him. And rightfully so. He made Mark look bad to his customers. It was probably an honest mistake, but it deserved a verbal lashing. That's life.

Well, Mark told me he never heard from this supplier again.

Never. Never ever.

He never called again.

I asked him: "Were you buying a lot of product from him?"

Mark   "About $4 million per year."
Me   "And how big was his company?"
Mark   "About $20 million."
        It was a massive percentage of this company's business!
Me   "And how long ago was this?"
Mark   "About four years."

So, $16 million in revenue lost, because this guy didn't have the confidence to pick up the phone after the customer told him he screwed up.

I asked him, "Do you need that product? That was a lot of product."

Mark   "I would *love* to have that product even now."
Me   "So why don't you call him?"

Mark, without skipping a beat: "It doesn't work that way. *He needs to call me.*"

At that point he could have dropped the mic and walked out of the room.

But there was no mic, just him and me sitting around his desk.

It doesn't work that way.

Don't wait for the customer to call you.

That's not their job (when it's not urgent).

You need to call them.

They *expect* you to.

They *want* you to.

Don't let it cost you millions of dollars.

"That's the first time anybody has called me on that damn thing!"

I was talking to the president of a large chemical distribution company.

He remarked that he had recently received a call from the new CEO of a large supplier of his.

He talked about how nice it was to get a phone call.

"Everybody just emails me," he said. "This guy called me on my cell phone and we had a great half-hour conversation!"

I asked him if he was angry that the guy called him on the phone.

"I prefer it," he said. "It's the first time anybody has ever called me on that damn thing!"

"Why is it better than email?" I asked him.

"Because we got to know each other. He was new, and now I know him. Nobody else called me. *He* called me."

Think that supplier has an advantage on the competition now?

I do too.

And that's the power of a phone call.

Nobody Calls Anymore

We assume that our customers get phone calls from their suppliers and partners all the time.

But think about your own days at the office: how many one-on-one phone calls do you get from your own suppliers?

You might have conference calls.

Or the supplier may call when there's something urgent or terrible happening.

But what about proactive "How are you? How's your family?" calls?

Not many, right?

How many in the last month?

Probably not even one, right?

We *assume* our customers are fighting off phone calls all day.

This is not true.

Your competition, because they are also human, deal with the exact same fears you do. And *they* are not reading this book (Well, most likely not.)

Want to stand out?

Pick up the phone.

Why Don't We Call?

I discussed why we don't pick up the phone in depth in Part I.

But if you skipped straight to the actions in this book: the short answer is fear.

We are afraid of upsetting the customer; imposing upon the customer; taking up the customer's time; annoying the customer. We are afraid of being rejected. We are afraid of failure. Ultimately, as I stated earlier in this chapter, the greatest fear is that we will lose the customer.

I said this in Part I, but it needs to be repeated here: *most salespeople's fear of rejection is apparently greater than our need to feed our families.* That is, we'd rather not call the customer than expose ourselves to the possibility being denied and rejected by them.

So we don't call.

That's why we don't call.

All the Good That Happens When We Call

Here's a list of all the goodness that you create when you pick up the phone:

- You are standing out from the crowd with this customer, because the competition is not using the phone like you are.

- Customers will be happy to hear from you. Once they get over their shock about you not needing anything from them, you will have a very pleasant conversation.

- You will have an opportunity to ask the customer what they are working on in a relaxed setting. And they will answer, arming you with information you would simply not have otherwise.

- You will be able to tell the customer about other products and services you can sell them to them.

- Your proactive phone call will demonstrate to the customer that you *care*—and that's really all customers want. We human beings want to know that the people we are working with care about us. It's not a whole lot more complicated than that. When you avoid the phone, you are demonstrating just the opposite!

- If you call a customer regularly, they *will* send you more business. Why? Because you're present. *You* will be in the front of their mind, not the competition. The backscratcher will have *your* name on it, not the competition's.

There is no downside to calling customers. Only great value to them and to you.

You Don't Increase Phone Hours by Trying to Spend More Hours on the Phone

When I increase salespeople phone hours from 4 hours to 8 or 10 hours per week for my clients, I don't do it by asking the salespeople to spend more hours on the phone.

I ask them to make more calls.

Remember, we focus on what we can control: the swing mechanics.

Picking up the phone and dialing a customer or prospect is something we can control.

But how many hours we spend on the phone is the opposite: it's not up to us. It depends on the availability of the person we are calling.

Instead, we measure quantities of phone calls.

How many proactive phone calls do you want to make this week? Five (one per day)? Ten? Twenty (four calls a day)? That's the goal. And then, whether you talk to the person or you leave a message—yes, we leave voicemails in the Selling Boldly approach to sales growth (more on this next)—it counts.

Quantity is the goal.

Because quantity allows us to control our fate.

Leave That Voicemail!

Many salespeople perceive leaving a voice message as a failure.

No!

You haven't failed anything!

It's exactly the opposite: you've succeeded! The customer got to hear your voice, and we know for a near fact that they are *not* hearing the competition's voice.

Here's a good voice message to leave:

"Tom, it's Alex Goldfayn. Listen, I was just thinking about you and wanted to pick up the phone. Nothing urgent, just wanted to catch up. If you have a few minutes, give me a call back. If I don't hear from you, I've got some time on Tuesday at 2 P.M., and I'll try again then. Look forward to catching up!"

As with the rest of our language, it's easy and light. There's no pressure here. In fact, I tell him there's nothing urgent. I tell him I was thinking about him. That's a compliment. I tell him I just want to catch up in general. I'm interested in what's happening with him. I'm present (the competition isn't). I care. I tell him the exact time and date I'll call him back if I don't hear from him. I've found some customers actually put that time and date on their calendar instead of calling me back, because for some reason that's easier for them. Go figure, but whatever works, right? But as soon as I tell him the date and time in that voicemail, it goes on my calendar, so I do it. I block off the time.

Create your own script, but leave it light. No pressure. No pushing. You're just thinking about them. You care.

Who knew leaving a message communicated all this?!

Leave the message!

SELLING BOLDLY	Applying the New Science of Positive Psychology to Dramatically Increase Your Confidence, Happiness, and Sales

PROACTIVE CALL PLANNER

Date Range:

What To Say On These Calls
- ➤ Just checking in.
- ➤ I was just thinking about you.
- ➤ How have you been?
- ➤ How's your family?
- ➤ What are you working on that I can help with?

Top Customers Who Can Buy More (And WHAT To Offer Them)	Customers I Haven't Talked To In Six Months Or More	Customers Who Used To Buy, But Stopped	Good Customers Who Just Received An Order (Follow-up)

Prospects I Once Talked To (3+ Months) But They Never Bought	Prospects I Know Are Buying Elsewhere Now	Prospects I've Never Talked To, But Want To Make Contact With	Prospects I'm Actively Speaking With, But Have Not Yet Bought

ALEX • GOLDFAYN
Get digital versions of this and other planners at www.goldfayn.com/Copyright 2018 Alex Goldfayn

Who to Call?

Use the "Proactive Call Planner" to lay out *who* you will call. You can fill out this monthly planner over a couple of weeks, as you wish, and then transfer over your weekly calls onto your "One-Page Sales Planner."

As you fill out this planner, I don't want the name of the company. List the names of *people* here. You're not having conversations with companies. You're speaking with people, so list the people.

There are eight different categories of contacts you can lay out here, half for customers you are already working with, and half for prospects who are not currently buying from you.

These are the categories:

1. Customers who currently buy from you, but can buy more from you. As you list the names here, also write down what other products they can buy from you. Your list would contain a name and additional product names or numbers, additional services, or additional quantities, which are also fair game.

2. Customers you haven't talked to in six months or more. This is an absolutely stellar list of people to call, and has resulted in many tens of millions of dollars in new sales for my clients over the years. Who's buying from you on autopilot? If there are customers you haven't talked to in at least six months, there is a very high chance they need more products and services from you. Call *them*.

3. Customers who used to buy, but stopped. Go back through your CRM, or your old emails, or your old contracts and invoices, and dig up a list of people who used to buy but no longer do. Reach out to them.

4. Good customers who just received products or services from you. Call them and do a post-delivery call (detailed in Chapter 34). Call them and ask if everything arrived in good shape. Ask if they're happy. Ask if there's anything else you can do. If not, pivot to another of our actions, like a did you know, or a reverse did you know, or a referral request.

5. Prospects you talked to, but they've never bought. Reach out again. Remind them about your conversation and that you're thinking about them.

6. Prospects you know are buying elsewhere. Think about your universe of potential customers. Make a list of people who are not buying from you, but *are* buying from your competition. Call them and tell them their lives would be better with *you*.

7. Prospects you've never talked to and wish to connect with. Who have you been *meaning* to call but have not done so yet?

8. Prospects you're actively engaged with, but have not yet bought. Give them a jingle. Remind them that you care, and you're present.

Is there some overlap here?

Sure, but who cares?

My goal is to give you some specific categories of contacts and prompt you to make a list of names you will call in the coming weeks or month.

Don't set this up for more than one month in advance.

A shorter time is okay (you can make a list that lasts two or three weeks, for example), but make a new one once the last one is a month old. Keep updating this list.

What to Say

This the fun part.

> Here is how to begin your proactive phone calls:
> "Hi Tom, it's Alex Goldfayn. Listen, I was just thinking about you, and wanted to pick up the phone and check in. How are you? What's happening?"

That's it.

That's really all you need to get started.

> If you've discussed family before, ask about them:
> "How's your family?"

Complicated, right?

And then, if the conversation is flowing well, and you're enjoying yourself, pivot very lightly and gently to the business at hand.

> "What are you working on these days?"

You're not pitching or selling or annoying or bothering with this question.

You're just inquiring about their work.

Most likely the customer or prospect will steer the conversation over to areas you can help them with.

Remember to ask your question, and be silent until the other person speaks.

Let them think.

They're not used to phone calls like this either.

In fact, one week into making these kinds of proactive phone calls, *you* will have far more experience with them than the customers and prospects you are calling.

Set the Calls Up If You Wish

I can hear you saying, "But my customers don't just sit by the phone."

Mine don't either.

So, about half the time, I like to set these up somewhat in advance.

If I have a cell phone relationship with my client, I will text them:

> "Hi Ryan, it's Alex. I was just thinking about you, and would love to catch up. Do you have some time today or tomorrow to speak for a few minutes?"

If I don't have their cell phone number (which means they're probably a prospect, because I have the cell phone numbers for nearly all my clients), I'll email the preceding script.

Here's why it works: it's short, easy, light, no-pressure, offers a compliment (I was thinking about you) and only asks for a few minutes. All that in a super-quick text. Ninety percent of the time, you'll find the answer is, "Good to hear from you, absolutely. How's 2 P.M.?"

Your Objections to Making Calls and My Responses

Allow me to list your top objections and discomfort at this moment, and react to them.

My customers and prospects don't want me to call.

This one comes up often in my client work.

First, although we frequently *assume* this, it is simply incorrect.

Second, we *may* have been told this before by customers who have asked us to email instead, but *only a few people have said this*. Maybe three or five, or at the most, 10 people. Right?

But we extrapolate it to many. Even though you have 50 or 100 or 200 customers, we assume that because *very few* customers have asked us not to call, the others don't want us to call either.

Don't make a strategy based on an exception. Let the exceptions be exceptions.

My customers and prospects don't have time to talk on the phone.

If the phone call is pleasant and enjoyable, and that's exactly what these are, they will *make* the time. And they'll remember the call fondly, weeks later. Just like the story earlier in this chapter with the chemical distribution company president who received a phone call from a supplier on his cell phone. He's crazy busy. But he was thrilled that a supplier called him.

My customers and prospects will be angry if I call.

I've taught thousands of salespeople to use the phone proactively in precisely the way I'm teaching you here, and *I can't think of one example of when the customer became angry when he or she got the call*. Not one. People don't get mad. Because they are human, and enjoy the incredibly rare no-stress interaction.

I don't have the time to make these calls.

Two thoughts on this one.

First, if you want to sell more and make more money, you can't afford *not* to make these calls. They are the best and easiest way for you to make more money.

Second, take a good, hard look at your week, and tell me honestly that you don't have, say, one 10-minute slot per day, every day, to make one phone call. Of course, you do. Everybody has 10 minutes. That's all we need here. Chances are you will be leaving a voicemail and now your 10 minutes will become 60 seconds.

26 | Always Ask for the Business

How many times has somebody been selling to you, and you're ready to go, ready to buy, you may even have your wallet in your hand, but the salesperson doesn't ask you for the business. So they leave your office without the sale. If only they would have asked, you would have bought. But they didn't. So you didn't.

We don't ask for the business regularly for the same reasons we don't pick up the phone: fear.

We don't want to be rejected.

And we don't want to offend.

But now that you know how good you are and how happy your customers are, and now that you understand the incredibly important role of confidence and boldness and optimism, it's time to start asking for the business every time you talk to somebody.

I'm asking you to pivot to the sale with every customer and prospect you talk to—even those who call in to place an order. Whether you call them or they call you, pivot to the sale.

The customer is spending time on the phone with you. They're interested in buying from you. You're interested in selling to them.

Ask for the business.

The worst that can happen is that they say no, and you're *precisely* where you were when you started the conversation. Nothing got worse.

There are two categories of pivots to the sale:

1. If you are talking to a customer or prospect about purchasing a new product or service, ask for the business.

2. If you have a longer sales cycle, or you feel the customer is truly not yet ready to buy, then pivot not to the business, but to the next commitment. The next phone call, or the next meeting or the next communication. Agree on the date and time that it will happen.

Here is the language.

Questions to Pivot to the Sale, and Ask for the Business

- Should we write it up?
- How many would you like?
- How would you like to pay?
- Our credit or yours?
- When can you get me the P.O.?
- When would you like these delivered by?
- I'll be in your area on Wednesday and Thursday. Which is better for you?
- I have a dozen in stock. How many do you want?
- Our prices go up next month. Would you like to lock in the current low prices?
- You've been ordering 100 monthly, but did you know there's a price break at 150?
- One hundred is good, but 200 is better!
- I have a little room on the truck. What do you want me to add to fill it up?
- I have it. Let's do something.
- If you order it today, I can guarantee delivery tomorrow.

- I have these available as singles and multiunit packs. Which is better for you?
- Want to increase to six units and apply the price break?
- Any questions before I enter your order?
- When can I expect payment for this?
- Can I transfer you to place the order?
- Ready?
- I can still ship it today if you place your order now.

If You Sell Services, Here Are Some Pivots to the Sale for You

- Should we begin?
- Are you ready to start?
- When do you want to meet?
- I'm excited to work with you. When do we begin?
- When can I expect the signed proposal back?
- I have some time for our kick-off call next week. Should we book it?
- I think I'm hearing you say you want to get started.
- I can meet the second or third week of the month to kick things off. Which is better for you?
- Anything else before we roll?

But if the customer is not yet ready to buy, you can pivot to the next commitment instead of the sale. This should probably always include a date and time.

Here Are Your Pivots to the Next Commitment

- I have time to speak on Monday and Wednesday. Which day is better for you?
- When do you want to talk next?

- So what's our next step?
- How would you like me to proceed?
- What do you want to do next?
- I'll put it on my calendar to reach out to you on Thursday. Will that be good?
- Okay, so you'll let me know where you are by the end of the week. If I don't hear from you by then, I'll call you on Monday afternoon. Does that sound okay?

That's 30 closing questions and seven pivots to the next commitment, all supplied by my clients when we do this exercise in client workshops. I go around the entire room and everybody contributes a closing question. So all of the preceding pivots came from salespeople like you. Also: my clients have successfully implemented these pivots. Which means they are used and we know they work.

Don't use them all.

Pick your favorite few.

Or create your own.

Then, go to your weekly "One-Page Sales Planner" and write out (or type out, if you're doing it digitally) your favorite pivot questions.

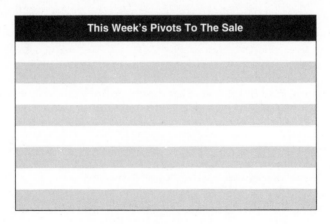

This Week's Pivots To The Sale

This way, they are in front of you.

Use them throughout your week.

Try them, test them, edit them. *Make them comfortable for you.*

Keep the ones that work, and ask them frequently.

If you have pivots on your planner that don't work, get them out, and replace them. Or not.

Focus on what's comfortable for you.

THE DYK PLANNER

DYK Complete List	DYK If/Then		DYK Top 10
	If The Customer Buys:	**If The Customer Buys:**	
	DYKs:	DYKs:	
	If The Customer Buys:	**If The Customer Buys:**	
	DYKs:	DYKs:	

ALEX • GOLDFAYN

27 | Tell Your Customers What Else They Can Buy from You

I know you sell to a lot of customers.

I know they buy a lot of different products.

But my research with more than 100 corporate clients and thousands of their salespeople shows that your customers know only about 20 percent of what they can buy from you.

Even if they have been buying from you for many years.

Even if they are some of your best and happiest customers.

Even if you've told them about your products and services.

Customers *still* only know about a small fraction of what they can buy from you. Which is pretty tragic, isn't it?

They would like to buy more from you. They love buying from you; that's why they've been with you for years.

You would like to sell more to them. You enjoy these customers, and it's certainly easier to help existing customers more than to go searching for new ones, isn't it?

But none of that is possible, because they don't know what else they can buy.

I repeat: *even if you told them, they do not know.*

How do I know they don't know?

How many times have you heard this terrible but honest statement from customers: "I didn't know you did that!"

And you say to them, "That's what you said a month ago when I told you about it the last time!"

Right?

Why is this?

Why don't customers know?

We tell them. They should know!

But they don't.

They don't know because they're busy.

They don't spend their days thinking about *your* stuff like you do. They think about *their* stuff. They have their own fires and problems and issues, and that's what they think about.

And this is also why I say it is impossible to overcommunicate.

You can't do it.

Customers Niche Us, and We Niche Them

Customers think of you as capable of selling to them *only* those products and services they have been buying from you for years.

Similarly, you discuss and offer them only those very same products and services. You rarely, if ever, offer them other products and services. (This is due to fear, as discussed in great depth in Part I. You're afraid of losing the customer. *If I offer them this other product, they might stop buying that product for which they've come to me for years.* Bird in the hand, right?)

The problem is that right now, today, they are buying products and services from the competition that they *could* be buying from you.

They would be better off buying these products and services from you.

But they can't. It's impossible. Because they don't know what else you can sell to them.

How to Tell Your Customers about What Else You Can Sell to Them

This is an incredibly simple technique I call the did you know question. DYK for short.

Ask your customers, "Did you know we can also help with *x*, or *y*, or *z?*"

Or: "Did you know we also have *x*, or *y*, or *z?*"

That's it. That's all the work needed.

Just ask people if they know how you can also help them or sell them something.

How to Ask This Question

In my previous book, *The Revenue Growth Habit,* I said you can drop these questions into existing conversations or pick up the phone to call somebody and tell them.

Having worked with scores of clients since then, and probably tens of thousands of did you know questions later, I can tell you that you really need only one of these approaches: inserting the did you know question during existing conversations should give you dozens of opportunities to ask the question weekly.

When a customer calls you with a problem or urgent matter, resolve it, and then ask your DYK.

"Anything else on that matter? Are you good? Great, listen, did you know we can also help with *x, y,* or *z?*"

That's it.

If a customer calls you with an order, add the DYK question.

"Would you like to add *x, y,* or *z* to that?"

Remember the bottle of water story from the introduction of this book? What's your bottle of water?

A Whopping 20 Percent of DYKs Close

Twenty percent of did you know questions result in the sale of an additional product or service! This is not a trivial number.

Ask five DYKs, close one.

Ask 20 DYKs, close four.

How many people at your company face customers?

Let's say there are 20 people.

If each of you ask five DYKs per day (that's about three seconds per question, and 15 seconds per day), you'll ask for 500 DYKs in a week, 2,000 per month, and 24,000 per year. With a twenty percent close rate, that's 4,800 new line items or sales. What's your median dollar amount per line item? $1,000? Welcome to $4.8 million in new money that you didn't have yesterday.

That's how this works.

Ask your DYKs!

Do YOU Know What You Can Sell to Your Customers?

During client workshops, I sometimes do a fascinating exercise with participants.

I ask people to write out as many of their own DYKs as they can in two minutes—as long a list as possible.

Then I have them split up into small groups to compare and discuss their lists. These are people from the same company.

Guess what happens?

The lists are often wildly different.

You can write out only so many items in two minutes. I do it this way because you have only a very short period of time to bring up these other products and services to your customers. There's pressure in those conversations. So I try to create pressure in the DYK list-making exercise too.

Well, what people find is that the lists differ a great deal from one person to the next.

Many times they say, *"I didn't even know we did that."*

So let me ask you: If *you* do not know the different ways you can help your customers, how can they?

How can you bring up products and services that you yourself are not thinking about?

The answer is they can't, and you can't.

So spend some time each week—a few minutes is enough—reviewing your line card. Or your website. Your catalog. Or your service lineup. Go over it, review it, marinate in it. Make a list.

Make a DYK Plan.

Use "The DYK Planner."

Planning Your DYKs

| SELLING BOLDLY | | Applying the New Science of Positive Psychology to Dramatically Increase Your Confidence, Happiness, and Sales |

THE DYK PLANNER

DYK Complete List	DYK If/Then		DYK Top 10
	If The Customer Buys: DYKs:	**If The Customer Buys:** DYKs:	
	If The Customer Buys: DYKs:	**If The Customer Buys:** DYKs:	

ALEX • GOLDFAYN

Here's how to use "The DYK Planner."

Think of this planner as a coach's play card. You know how NFL coaches stand on the sidelines with a laminated play call sheet with color and highlights? They read the plays from this card into their headsets, which the quarterback hears in his helmet. This planner is *your* coach's play card.

Column 1: The DYK Complete List

Make a complete list of common products and services you can bring up to your customers. Be inclusive. Unbundle them, meaning don't list categories of products but individual products and services. Don't assume your customers know. They do not. So this column is your all-inclusive list.

Columns 2 and 3: DYK If/Then

In this section, there is room for four if/then lists. Here's how they work.

On the top row of each of the four tables, write down a major product or service your customers frequently buy from you. Underneath, list some DYK products they probably need from you if they also buy that product.

For example, for a distributor of pipes and valves, you might list a ball valve as a major product customers may buy, and underneath that you'd list the DYKs: pipes, fittings, glue, O-rings, and so on.

Or, for an insurance agency, you might list auto insurance as the major product in the first row, and under that, write out your DYKs: home insurance, umbrella coverage, jewelry, liability, business errors and omissions, and so forth.

Like that.

So, in each of the four tables, you'd list a common product people buy, and DYKs you should ask them if they buy that product.

Repeating products in the four lists is okay.

Column 4: DYK Top 10

Now, bring over your top 10 DYK items over to this right column. Now you have your top 10 DYKs, in a single quick reference.

How to Use This Planner

Fill out "The DYK Planner" monthly, but transfer the DYKs from here onto your "One-Page Sales Planner."

Keep this planner in front of you throughout the month.

Print it, highlight it if you'd like, laminate it if you wish, but keep it where your eyes can see it.

The biggest downfall of making lists is that they are useless if they are not in front of you.

Don't keep this in a computer window buried under six other windows.

Keep it where you can see it.

More DYKs = More Sales

The more DYKs you ask, the more you will sell.

The more DYKs your colleagues ask, the more your company will grow.

If you can, get your fellow salespeople involved in this pursuit.

DYKs are a fantastic communications tool for customer service and inside salespeople too. They're on the phone all day. A three-second DYK is a spectacularly effective tool for them.

Ask DYKs as much as you can, and ask your colleagues to do the same.

And sales will have no choice but to grow.

28 | Let Your Customers Tell You What Else They Buy

In the previous chapter, we covered DYKs, and asked you to propose products and services to customers and prospects.

In this chapter, we discuss an extraordinarily powerful question that has customers and prospects *tell you* what else they need. It's incredibly simple and creates tremendous results.

It's called the reverse did you know question, or rDYK in shorthand.

Here's the question.

> "What else are you buying elsewhere that I might be able to help you with?"

You know the crazy thing about that question?

Like all of the other communications in this section, if you ask them, they will tell you!

They'll tell you what they're buying from the competition.

They'll tell you what else they need that they are not getting from you.

Here are some more versions of this question.

> "What are you having trouble sourcing that I can help you with?"
>
> "What do you have going on that we're not working together on? I'd like to help you with that."
>
> "What do you buy that you'd like to bring over to me?"

How to Plan These

Because the customer is telling *us* what she needs, there's no product planning or listing here. Just write up the customers you will ask. Do this on the weekly "One-Page Sales Planner."

Use the space on the backside of the planner to list the names and companies of the people you will ask this question.

This Week's rDYKs
Name & Co

Think about who you might interact with this week—calls that are scheduled or calls you're planning to make or meetings you might have this week, and list the people who you know are buying other products and services elsewhere.

Make your list, and ask people throughout the week. But also, *ask people you talk to who are not on this list.*

Give yourself the flexibility to ask rDYKs—and also our other communications—to people beyond your plan. Just drop them into conversations. You don't know who is going to call, but you do know a lot more people will call than you have on your list. So remain open to asking them as well.

29 | Following Up Will Make You Rich

So your customer asked you for a quote or proposal.

You dropped everything and worked on it.

You sent it to him.

If he doesn't say yes right away, he will probably remain silent.

That's because people don't like to say *no*. They avoid it. It may be hard to believe, because in our profession we get rejected all the time, but people really don't enjoy making the rejection.

Consider all the quotes or proposals you've sent over the last month or year.

It's likely that at least 50 percent of the people receiving them were silent.

These are people we need to follow up with.

The following process closes 20 percent of the outstanding quotes and proposals for my clients.

Do I have your attention?

And that's if you send all three of the follow-ups by email.

If you replace the middle email with a phone call, you will close *30 percent of your outstanding quotes and proposals.*

Interested?

In this chapter, I teach you exactly what I teach my clients.

I give you the communications tools here.

But you have to make them. That's the only thing I can't do.

Not only do you need to make the communications, they must be done systematically.

As in, repeatedly and systematically, discussed in the first chapter of this part of the book.

So You've Sent a Quote or Proposal

Here are your follow-ups.

Within 24 Hours, Send the First Email

"Tom, just a quick follow-up on that quote we discussed yesterday. I sent it as promised. I just want to make sure it got to you because these things tend to get picked off by spam filters. Did you get it?"

One line: write it out once and then copy and paste it forever.

This is your quick check-in.

You just want to know it got there.

If they don't reply to this one, move on to your next communication.

The Second Follow-Up

"Tom, I haven't heard from you. I sent that quote you asked for. I was just wondering, where are you on that? I'm looking forward to helping you with it."

One line. Copy, paste, send.

Nice and easy.

No pressure.

You're just wondering.

If he doesn't reply to either of these two follow-ups, he's just being rude.

He asked *you* for the quote.

You sent it to him.

Then you followed up twice.

He can't bring himself to reply?

I am annoyed *for you!*

Send the third and final f/u (that's short for "follow-up!").

The Third and Final Follow-Up

"Tom, I sent the quote the day we talked about it, and I've followed up twice. Listen, the quote is expiring in 48 hours, so if you'd like to move forward with this, please let me know in the next two days. If not, I look forward to coming together on something else soon! Thank you!"

Just like that.

And you will find that some people will reply and say, "No, no, no, wait, wait, wait . . ." And they will buy. But they needed a deadline.

What's that, you say? Your quotes or proposals don't have an expiration date?

Add one.

It's not fair to you to leave these hanging out there in the ether for months.

If somebody comes back to you after their quote expires, you can always make an exception if you choose.

But you need to plan your life and your products.

These three follow-ups will close another 20 percent of your outstanding quotes.

And, as I said earlier, if you replace the middle email with a phone call, you'll increase this close rate to 30 percent.

That's a massive increase in closed quotes and proposals.

The System Is the Key

Here's the best way to implement this.

Put all three follow-ups on your calendar when you send the quote. Do it right away. If it's on your calendar, there's a better chance of it happening.

Here's another way: have an administrative assistant do all the following up. You send the quote, copy this assistant, and he or she calendars and executes the follow-ups.

The key is to follow up all the time. Regularly and systematically.

You've done the work.

You've sent the quote.

Now go get what's yours!

30

Sell with Your Testimonials: Show Your Prospects How Happy Your Customers Are

In Part III, we discussed in depth how to get testimonials.

But what do you do once you have them?

Now what?

You can have hundreds or even thousands of wonderful testimonials, but if nobody sees them, they are of no value. They are like a tree falling in the forest: nobody *knows* about your happy customers.

We have to share these testimonials. They must be out in the world where they can help others decide if they should buy from us.

Basically, *everything that leaves your office would be made more powerful with a testimonial.* They make everything stronger. Testimonials make everything truer. It is the customer saying you are wonderful, which is quite different from *you* saying you are wonderful. Put them everywhere. In fact, if you have a catalog or a brochure, put them on every page!

What the Testimonials Should Look Like

Here are four guidelines for how to display your testimonials:

1. If your customers give you permission to share their testimonials—and the vast majority will—use names, titles, and company names. If you're not using them already, I'm wondering why not. If the customer did not give you permission, and you feel their testimonial would be helpful to share anyway, obviously follow the agreement you have with your customer and anonymize the testimonial as they allowed.

2. One or two sentences are enough. And it's okay to mix and match sentences, maybe one from the beginning of the conversation and one from the middle or end. You're not a newspaper reporter; you're communicating the words of a happy customer.

3. Don't worry about repeating testimonials. Nobody will care. You may worry about it but your audience—even if they realize that *this* testimonial appears on your website *and* in your catalog—won't think twice about it. It's normal. It's what you're supposed to do.

4. Like everything else we're doing here, don't overthink it. Don't try to pick the *perfect* testimonial. Just pick a testimonial and put it where people can see it.

Active and Passive Testimonial Sharing

You can share testimonials actively and passively. That is, we can place them directly in front of people we are selling to (that's active), or we can put them places where people may see them when they consume our other material (this is the passive way). They are both highly effective, but active communication will make you more money, and faster—so let's talk about that one first.

Active Testimonial Sharing

By Email

You can share testimonials by email, on the phone, or during a meeting or presentation. Let's go through all three. Sharing testimonials like this has generated a lot of money for my clients.

Like all of these communications, it's incredibly simple, but requires some confidence and boldness. Following is the email draft.

"Tom, we have a customer similar to you, and here is what she has to say about us:

<*Paste Testimonial Here*>

<*Name, Title, Company*>

"I'd like to help *you* this way. I can talk on Tuesday or Thursday about bringing you this kind of value. Which do you prefer?"

You can send this testimonial by email, or you can communicate when you speak with your customer.

Here's what the email looks like, including the testimonial.

"Tom, we have a customer similar to you, and here is what they have to say about us:

"Of my 50 vendors, Artistic Carton would be within the top five. I don't really know who would be ahead of them. It is 20 to 30 percent faster [for us] to work with Artistic Carton. With them, there is less back and forth. Pete just says let me know what it is and we'll take care of it."

—Jill Smith, product manager, XYZ Distributor

[This is excerpted from an actual client testimonial I pasted in from the Chapter 19 transcript.]

I'd like to help *you* this way. I can talk on Tuesday or Thursday about bringing you this kind of value. Which do you prefer?

Copy and paste the first and last lines from the draft, and copy and paste the testimonial, and then you click "send." It's a 30-second action, with incredibly powerful results. If I'm the prospect, here's a *peer* of mine, with similar problems and challenges—and wins—saying that you are one of her very best vendors. And not only that but you save her a quarter of her time?! You bet I'm replying to this email. How many emails like this do you think people get? Remember, the purpose of *all* these communications is to be in front of customers and prospects in ways that your competition isn't.

In Conversation

If you're on a call with a customer who is considering placing a new order, or a prospect who has not yet purchased, it's a perfect time to share a testimonial.

> "Tom, we have a customer similar to you, a product manager at XYZ Distribution, and she recently told me that we're one of her very best suppliers, out of 50, and also that working with us saves her 20 to 30 percent of her time. Now I'd like to help you this way, and if we move forward, I'll be able to! Ready to roll?"

In this example, I used the sharing of the testimonial as a pivot to the sale.

But if it's earlier in the process, say, with a prospect, you can simply pivot to a phone call.

> ". . . I'd like to help you this way also. I can talk about it on Wednesday or Friday. What's good for you?"

Again, *nobody* does this except my clients. So, chances are, you'll be the only one your customer hears this from . . . ever!

During Sales Meetings

Many of my clients use these testimonials during their meetings.

They print them and pass them out if there are multiple people in the room.

Then, if there is a slide deck presentation, they put the testimonials on the screen, and *read* them to the people in the room. That way, their audience *sees* the testimonials and *hears* them too, cementing them into the brains that are around the table.

If three people are making a presentation, how many do you think are sharing powerful testimonials like this?

During Trade Shows

A lot of my clients attend trade shows. For some, it's their main avenue for getting new customers.

What do exhibitors do at a trade show?

They talk about their products and services, right?

Walk around a trade show, looking at exhibits and displays, and what do you see?

Products everywhere. Services. Specifications. Details. Functionality. You know, boring commodity stuff. Everybody's setup looks similar. It's all really quite bland and boring this way.

I teach my clients to differentiate simply.

Here's a powerful approach: communicate less about your products and services and more about your *happy* customers.

- Put testimonials on your background display. In addition to the many product pictures that I'm sure are currently there, create some areas for testimonials, complete with names and companies.

- Create testimonial handouts and give them to people. Think packets, postcards, one-sheets, books, pins, anything. The vehicle doesn't matter. Just put testimonials into people's hands.

- When you do this, review some of the testimonials with the attendees. Use a finger to guide their eye through the testimonial, and read pieces of it aloud. Then say, "Let us do this for you." That's the key: allowing the customer to imagine herself also being happy like this (more on this shortly).

- Just talk about your happy customers, and summarize testimonials. "My customer at a similar company recently told me that . . ."

Don't Underestimate the Power of Aspiration That These Testimonials Create

There is nothing *you* can say that is more effective, more powerful, more dramatic, more emotional, more connecting, or truer than the testimonial of a happy customer.

To this end, seeing a testimonial is incredibly powerful for a prospect.

This is what you get: "Wow, I want *that* too."

Remember that most suppliers or providers aren't as good as you are.

They let their customers down.

Customers are frustrated.

On most days, your customers are unhappy with at least one or more of their suppliers; probably more.

And then here you come, with these shiny, happy people singing your praises.

They're so pleased!

You're reliable!

You do what you say!

You save them a quarter of their time! What?!

Your prospects will want that too. They will pay you good money for it.

Your Objection and My Response

If you've made it to this part of the chapter, you are probably feeling the following resistance: *If I share my customers' names and companies, my competition will pick them off and steal them from me.*

Has this occurred to you?

I know about this, because it almost always comes up in my speeches and client meetings.

Here is the my response: *The competition is already calling on your customers every day, and yet they stay with you.*

Remember what's happening here: the customer has poured cement on their relationship with you. They have said, "I love working with you, and yes, you can tell this to the world."

And you have poured cement on your relationship with the customer by telling them they are one of your best customers.

Here's the truth: *Most* of the competition will be too frightened to call a customer who is on your website. They know he is a very happy customer.

Second, let's say they do call. Your customer is *incredibly happy*. So much so that his testimonial is on your materials!

He's not going anywhere.

In over a decade of doing this work, with hundreds of clients and thousands and thousands of customer interviews—and tens of thousands of testimonials shared publicly—I don't know of a single example of a customer being poached because his testimonial was shared. Not one.

This objection we are discussing is rooted in *our* fear. The same fear that keeps us from picking up the phone, asking for the business, and doing the good work of helping our customers more.

So don't worry about it.

Go tell the world how happy your customers are.

The world, and all of your prospects in it, deserve to know!

31

"What Percent of Your Business Do We Have?"

Many of your customers do not send you all of their business in your product or service category.

So, let's ask them about that.

> "Tom, what percent of your business would you guess we have?"
>
> For our example here, let's say the answer is 20 percent.
>
> "Interesting. I'd like to get that up to 30 percent. What would that look like? I like working with you. You're one of my favorite customers. Let's see about helping you some more."

For the customer, this is a small movement in business.

He needs to move only 5 percent of what he buys from one supplier, and 5 percent from another supplier, over to you.

But for you, this is a 50 percent increase in business with this customer.

Do this 10 or 20 times over, and it gets interesting.

Why Would the Customer Give You This Information?

That's what clients ask me when we discuss this technique.

They tell you because they consider you a valued partner.

Because they appreciate your work, and what you do for them.

You are reliable and dependable, and they are happy to help you serve them better.

That's what my clients find when they ask this question and their customers answer.

Your customer will tell you.

And then you can ask for a little bit more. Because you're interested in helping this customer more.

And sometimes, about a third to half of the time, they'll give it to you.

Just because you asked.

So, let's ask!

REFERRAL PLANNER

Date Range:

How To Ask For Referrals

➤ Who do you know, like yourself, who would benefit from working with me the way that you do?
➤ Would you like to connect us, or should I reach out and use your name?
➤ I know you're busy; so that I don't jump the gun, when do you think you might get to that?
➤ Excellent; so if I don't hear from you by then, I'll check in. Does that sound okay?

Who To Ask For INTERNAL Referrals	Who To Ask For EXTERNAL Referrals

Referral Results			
Referral From	Who	How	When

ALEX • GOLDFAYN
Get digital versions of this and other planners at www.goldfayn.com/Copyright 2018 Alex Goldfayn

32

People Love Giving Referrals—But We Hate Asking

As discussed early on in this book, people love to give referrals.

We know this because when we ask a group of people we are with for a referral, they trip over one another making a case for *their* person.

Think about your own experience: if a friend asks for a good handyman or plumber, and you have one, aren't you happy to recommend your person? Not only this, but you make a *case* for your provider. You *fight* for them.

People love to recommend good, trusted suppliers, service providers, and partners.

It's just that we don't ask. Because of fear. Which we dealt with in Part I.

Why Customers Love to Give Referrals

Here are the top reasons our customers love to give referrals:

- They get to help a friend.
- They get to help you.
- It affirms their decision. *I made a great choice. You should too!*

225

- Along these lines, making a referral feeds the ego. *Do I have a guy for you!*
- I refer somebody to you, and they buy from you, and then tomorrow I need something urgently—you'll kind of *owe me one,* won't you? So I will come to you and ask you for a favor. And you will feel like you need to prioritize me ahead of the others that day. As you should. I just did you a solid, and now you'll feel like repaying it.

There Are Two Different Kinds of Referrals

You can ask for two different kinds of referrals:

1. **Internal referrals:** This is a request to be connected to another buyer of your products or services *within* this company. Many of you sell to large companies where more than one person can buy what you sell. If you sell for a manufacturer, sometimes there are a dozen or more people who can buy your stuff, especially if distributors are among your customers. So here we ask for the others. We are looking for their colleagues inside the company.
2. **External referrals:** These are usually customers or suppliers of your customer, but also friends, family, acquaintances, association or chamber of commerce colleagues, executive group peers, and so forth. There is no shortage of people to connect you with someone from outside each customer's company.

How to Ask for a Referral

Here is your language for asking for an ***internal*** referral.

"Tom, who do you know like yourself at your company who would get the same kind of value from working with me as you do?"
Or . . .
"Tom, who do you know like yourself at your firm who I can help like I help you?"
Or . . .

> "Tom, who do you work with there who also buys what I sell?"
> Or, you can get even more specific . . .
> "Tom, who do you work with at the St. Louis office [or any branch you want to get into] that I could also help like I help you?"

And here is how to ask for an *external* referral.

> "Tom, who do you know like yourself, at another company, who I can help like I help you?"
> Or . . .
> "Tom, who do you work with who's a customer or a supplier who would get similar value as you do from working with me?"
> Or . . .
> "Tom, who do you know from the associations or peer groups you belong to who could benefit from working with me the way that you do?"

Once you ask, do not speak until the customer answers your question. Remember, silence is money (Chapter 23).

Count numbers or sheep, forward or backward, it doesn't matter. And *be comfortable with this.*

The Who, the How, and the When

I ask for a referral from my clients in many of my speeches and workshops.

They are not aware I will be asking in front of the room.

I ask one of the preceding questions, and here is what happens: at first, they panic. You can *see* it. But I stay quiet. Then you can see them start thinking about it. Then they consider their options. I don't talk. I am comfortable. I just look at them. The audience is looking between me and the client, usually the owner or CEO or a high-level executive at their company. Then, 99 out of 100 times, they think of somebody!

"Well, I know John Jackson, who runs a lumber distributorship that we sell to," they say.

Now I have the *Who*.

But we're not done yet. This is not a good referral yet.

"Would you like to send an email connecting us, or should I just reach out and use your name? What's better for you?"

That's a key, critical question.

I need to know how I should communicate with this person.

Otherwise, it's all nebulous. What should I do? What will the referrer do? We need to make this concrete and understood by both parties.

Ask that question in the preceding box, and then *be silent again*.

The vast majority of people, nine times out of 10, will say they would like to connect to you. Why? Because *they want the credit for the referral. They want their contact to know they are making a good connection for them!* Like I said earlier in this chapter, ego is a big part of why people give referrals.

Once they say how they want to proceed, you have the *How*. But you're not done yet! There is one more question.

"Great, so I'll wait for you to connect us. So that I don't jump the gun, when do you think you might get to it. I know you're busy . . ."

Then, you guessed it: close your mouth and breathe.

The customer will say, "Next week," or "Friday," or some other day.

Now you have the *When*.

But there's still one more step—summarize for understanding and to make a referral agreement with your customer.

"Great. You'll send an email connecting me to John by the end of next week, which I appreciate a great deal because this is how I feed my kids. If I don't hear from you by then, I'll give you a call the following Monday to check in, okay?"

And they will agree 100 percent of the time. Now you have your referral agreement.

Immediately put your date of follow-up onto your calendar so you don't forget. If you say you will do something, be totally sure you will do it. Doing what you promise will always set you apart from 90 percent of the competition instantly. It's not that hard to be better than the competition, which is not very good.

And that is how you ask for a referral.

You need the *who*, the *how*, and the *when*. Then summarize everything in a sentence and commit to following up.

The entire interaction should take about one minute, if that.

The Finer Points of Referral Asking

So, let's review what's happening in this referral language:

- Always start with, "**Who** do you know," not "Do you know somebody?" The former asks people to think of a name. The latter is a yes or no question.

- I know this is repetitive, but it's so important that it deserves frequent repetition: too many referrals are lost to nervous chatter. Ask for a referral and then be silent until the customer thinks of somebody.

- Once you get a name, ask your customer how they wish to connect you—by email, copying you both—or perhaps some other way. Maybe they want to have a conference call. About a week before writing this very chapter, a good client of mine came to a breakfast meeting where he introduced me to the CEO of his bank. Or would the customer prefer that you simply reach out to his contact and use his name?

- Once the *how* is set, get a timing commitment. When can they get to it? Then commit to following up shortly after this.
- Finally, summarize everything the customer just committed to.

Using the Selling Boldly "Referral Planner"

SELLING BOLDLY	Applying the New Science of Positive Psychology to Dramatically Increase Your Confidence, Happiness, and Sales

REFERRAL PLANNER

Date Range: _____

> Who do you know, like yourself, who would benefit from working with me the way that you do?
> Would you like to connect us, or should I reach out and use your name?
> I know you're busy; so that I don't jump the gun, when do you think you might get to that?
> Excellent; so if I don't hear from you by then, I'll check in. Does that sound okay?

Who To Ask For INTERNAL Referrals	Who To Ask For EXTERNAL Referrals

Referral Results			
Referral From	Who	How	When

ALEX • GOLDFAYN

Create a new referral planner at least monthly, but more frequently if you find yourself working through them quickly.

This sheet has a planning component on top, and a tracking component on the bottom, reminding you to get your *who, how,* and *when.*

At the top, sit down for two minutes and think which of your customers you can ask for internal referrals, and also which ones you can request external referrals from.

Then, simply ask for them.

Track your results: Who did you ask? Who did they refer? How will they connect you? And when will this happen?

You can transfer these names to "The One-Page Sales Planner" to incorporate the referral requests into your schedule.

Just ask the three questions in the who, how, and when boxes in this chapter, and you will have more referrals than you will know what to do with.

33

The Power of Handwritten Notes

I have a handwritten note on my desk, and it has been there for years. I keep a clean desk, but the note stays. Since I have received the note, I have changed desks and also we have moved homes. And yet, the note stays on top of my desk, over to the edge on the right side. It's important to me. It's from a woman who attended one of my talks and took the time to write me a detailed note, on a full-size piece of stationery, about how it affected her. It makes me feel good. So it stays.

I have another one in my car. I keep it in my center console, and I read it when I'm grouchy.

"You Would Have Lost Us if You Hadn't Sent This Note"

Recently, I was working with a large manufacturer's customer-facing staff.

We'd been working together for about four months, and this was a follow-up workshop with the large group to discuss successes, wins, and progress.

One of the salespeople raised his hand and told this story.

He had made a terrible mistake on an order. He sent the wrong product, and it got there late.

The customer was rightfully angry, and explained his displeasure in great detail. With choice words.

The salesman went about fixing the problem, just as you would.

He corrected the order, made sure it was delivered, and followed up with the customer.

Then he sent a handwritten note.

About a month later, when he came to visit the customer, the CEO walked out of his office, holding the handwritten note.

But the salesman had not sent the note to the CEO!

He sent it to his purchasing contact.

The CEO said, "This note started with our purchasing agent, then it went to his manager, and it worked its way around to all of the people who were affected by your mistake. And it landed on my desk."

He paused, and then concluded: *"If you hadn't sent this note, you would have lost us."*

And *there* is the power of a handwritten note.

Why Handwritten Notes Are So Effective

Do you remember the last handwritten note you received, when it wasn't your birthday or Christmas?

Most people can remember.

Because that's how rare it is to get one these days.

In a world of email, social media, and text messages, a handwritten note is a glorious relic of a slower, simpler time. People *love* to get them.

They are hugely memorable.

They have massive staying power.

They are incredibly simple to write, and enjoyable for both the sender and the recipient.

They show the customer that you are not only thinking of them, but thinking of them over an extended period of time.

For these reasons, they are highly effective with the recipient, who is, presumably in our case, a customer or prospect.

Find a Routine for Your Notes

Every Friday at around 2 P.M., I sit down at my desk and write three to five handwritten notes. This takes me no more than 30 minutes.

I like to write with fountain pens, so I go to my pens, and select one.

Then I pick an ink and a sheet of paper.

I enjoy the process.

Fountain pens are a hobby for me, so this routine allows me to enjoy my hobby.

I sit and think about who I interacted with this week who I want to send a nice note to.

Then I pick the first three to five people who come to mind.

And I write a note about something we talked about. Family or sports or a challenge, or wine or food, or a vacation or a car. Whatever it might have been. I write about that.

I can tell you that nearly everybody I sent a handwritten note to brings it up to me later, explaining how nice it was to get one.

Send Human Notes, Not Thank-You Notes

Don't send thank-you notes because everybody who sends notes sends thank-you notes.

That's really the only kind there are.

What's rare is a *human* note.

One that references something you talked about with the customer.

For example: *I hope your daughter's move into her new college went well. That must have been really difficult for you guys, but you must be so proud.*

Or: *How was the game? I bet you enjoyed the tailgating beforehand. That's one of my favorite things to do with my dad when we go to football games together.*

Like that.

It's okay to say thank-you in these notes, but don't make that the main point.

And don't bring up business.

The customer will do that for you.

34 | The Post-Delivery Call

A great time to call a customer is after a product or service is delivered.

This is a check-in phone call.

You're calling to see if everything went well and asking if your customer is happy.

My clients really enjoy this communication because there's no sales pressure. It's pleasant. And, like the other actions in this section, the competition rarely, if ever, makes calls like this. In fact, one of my clients calls this an "after-action call"—you're just checking in to make sure everything went okay.

Here's the first part of this communication.

> "Tom, it's Alex. Listen, I'm just checking in. Did you get that shipment as discussed? Did everything go okay? You're good? Great . . ."

That's part one.

Let's talk about what you're doing here with an inquiry like this:

- You're showing the customer you care.
- You're showing them you're thinking about them.
- As such, you're showing them they are important to you.
- You're separating yourself from the competition.
- You're creating a positive interaction. The customer is likely happy. And if he is not, you're creating an opportunity to *preemptively* fix a problem, without the customer needing to call. They will be extremely grateful for this.

If the customer is positive, and pleased, continue to part two, which is a pivot to any of our communications.

"Great, listen, did you know we can also help you with this other product, and we're just as good at that one?"

Or:

"Great, what else are you buying elsewhere that I may be able to help you with?"

Or:

"Who do you know like yourself who I can help like I help you?"

You can pivot to any of our quick and easy communications here.

Nice and easy.

You're just helping the customer.

This works particularly well if the customer is happy and responds affirmatively to the first part of this inquiry.

You're just being present.

You're showing the customer you care.

And you're asking if they'd like some more of this kind of care.

35

Putting It All Together with the "The One-Page Sales Planner"

Let's talk about the system.

Take a look at "The One-Page Sales Planner."

It's a two-sided sheet, where all of your planning and actions come together to take you through a powerful sales-growing week.

SELLING BOLDLY

Applying the New Science of Positive Psychology to Dramatically Increase Your Confidence, Happiness, and Sales

THE ONE-PAGE SALES PLANNER

> This week, I will help more people more.
> My customers deserve more of my great value!

Name:

Date Range:

Code	Action
Call	Proactive Call
PTS	Pivot to the Sale (Ask for the Business)
DYK	Did You Know Question
rDYK	Reserve Did You Know Question
QF/U	Quote or Proposal Follow-Up
% Biz	% of Business Question
Ref	Ask for a Referral
Comm T	Communicate a Testimonial Proactively
HWN	Hand-Written Note
PDC	Post Delivery Call

This Week's Pivots To The Sale

Day	Proactivity Tally	Actions	Results Action, Customer, Outcome	Revenue Estimated/Est. Annual/ Quoted/Sold
Monday				
Tuesday				
Wednesday				
Thursday				
Friday				

"Whether you think you can, or you think you can't, you're right!" - Henry Ford

ALEX • GOLDFAYN Get digital versions of this and other planners at www.goldfayn.com/Copyright 2018 Alex Goldfayn

---

SELLING BOLDLY

Applying the New Science of Positive Psychology to Dramatically Increase Your Confidence, Happiness, and Sales

Proactive Call List		This Week's DYKs		This Week's Quote Follow Ups	This Week's Referral Requests	
Name & Company	C or P	Name & Company	Product/Service	Name & Company	Name & Company	In/Ex

This Week's Hand-Written Notes

Name & Company

This Week's Top Revenue-Potential PROSPECTS	This Week's rDYKs	This Week's Testimonial Communications	
Name & Company	Name & Company	To Name & Company	Whose Testimonial

This Week's Post-Delivery Calls

Name & Company

This Week's Top Revenue-Potential CUSTOMERS

Name & Company

Get digital versions of this and other planners at www.goldfayn.com/Copyright 2018 Alex Goldfayn

Fill out this planner for next week at the end of the day Friday, or Sunday or Monday morning.

Here's how to leverage this planner into sales growth.

Start on the Planning Side

- Start with your two- to four-week planners discussed earlier in this book and bring over your top-priority actions.

- Write out your top priority DYKs, rDYKs, quote follow-ups, testimonial communications, referrals to request, handwritten notes to send, and post-delivery calls to make.

Key point here: write the names of the people you will call and their companies. Don't limit these lists to just companies. We want to think about the people. Our relationships are with the humans. We *help* the people.

For your DYK list, write down the customer's name and also the product you will suggest.

For testimonial communications, write down who you will communicate the testimonials to and *whose* testimonials you will send.

For the referral requests, write down who you will ask and whether you will ask for an internal referral or an external referral.

- Next, looking at these lists, head to the lower left, and write out this week's top revenue-potential prospects and customers.

- Finally, review the lists again, and in the upper left, write out your proactive call list. Indicate a *C* if the person is a customer, and a *P* if a prospect.

Now Turn the Page to the Schedule Side

1. First, go to Chapter 26, review the list of pivots to the sale, and write down your favorite ones for this week in the space on the upper right of the front side of this page. These are the closing questions you will use during your conversations this week.

2. Next, plan your week by transferring a few actions and customers and prospects from the other side of this planner. What will you do on Monday? Will you ask for a referral? Or write a note? What about Tuesday? Maybe that's a day for two or three proactive calls. Use the codes in the key at the top to save space.

3. Track your results. Write down if you did the action or not, and what happened:

   Who was the recipient of your action?

   What action did you do?

   What was the outcome? How did it go? (Remember, not succeeding is perfectly okay. *That's* not up to us. But not asking is not okay. That's in the swing mechanics. We control that.)

4. In the revenue column, write down your estimated dollar value of this effort, if it results in a sale. I want you to start connecting your communications with sales dollars.

   Just take a shot here if you're pre-quote. What do you think this DYK product or referral opportunity might be worth to you in terms of revenue?

   If you're at the quote stage, right down the dollar figure.

   If you've sold it, of course, write down the amount.

5. Finally, use the Proactivity Tally column, on the left hand side of the table to place a tick mark every time you execute one of the proactive communications on your planner. You can implement actions that you did not plan; that's okay. But also do the ones you did prepare for. Then do more!

Like the other planners, keep this one where you can see it. It's of no use if it's buried under a stack of papers, or hiding behind 14 windows on your computer screen.

Plan.

Communicate.

Sell.

Enjoy life.

36

For Owners, CEOs, Executives, and Managers: This Is How to Implement Selling Boldly at Your Company

If you are a CEO, president, or division leader with profit and loss oversight, or a department manager, this chapter is for you. It is about how to implement the Selling Boldly system throughout your organization.

When I start working with new clients, I tell them that this is basically a behavior change project. We want people to *do* some new things. These things are, basically, all communications. We want people to communicate more with customers and prospects. That's the work. But to change behavior, as discussed in depth in this book, we need to change thinking also. We are working to get your customer-facing staff to know how good they are (that's the thinking change), and then to behave accordingly (that's the communicating more).

So we're working to create some change. The problem is most people don't like change. They don't like doing new things. Change is uncomfortable. As a rule, people are wired to resist change. But making change with salespeople, who are probably the most independent employees in most organizations, is the hardest thing of all.

Nobody Likes Change

In fact, salespeople are much better at avoiding change than leaders are at implementing change. That's because, throughout their careers, they have learned that most changes do not stick. *If I avoid this long enough, it will also go away.* Like nearly all of the other changes that the boss has tried to implement over the years. You can't blame salespeople for this. Most change comes and quickly goes. It's what their experience has taught them.

And, so, when you announce a big change in the sales approach, like those detailed in this book, the following passes through their minds:

- "It's just another flavor of the month for the boss."
- "Let's see if we're still talking about this *next* month."
- "I don't have time for this."
- "We don't need this."
- "This won't work for us."
- "I know how to sell. I'm talking to customers all day long. Are you?"

In each case, the main issue is fear (see Part I). Fear of the unknown. Fear of having to learn something new. Fear of working harder. Fear of working more. Fear of the implication that the status quo hasn't been enough. *They think I'm not pulling my weight around here.* Fear of the discomfort this new work might cause.

But the good news is that we can overcome this discomfort and resistance and implement organizational change effectively.

How to Implement Change with Customer-Facing People Effectively

Change must come from the top. If it isn't important to the owner or the CEO or the division chief, it isn't going to be important to the managers or the frontline people. Change that starts in the middle levels of your company is nearly impossible to implement because it doesn't have the energy of top leadership or the commitment of the staff. Staff must know that the change is important to the leadership.

Accountability is required. In fact, there must be systems for account-ability. Tools for planning and measuring the new behaviors should be created and used. Furthermore, managers' feedback should be systematic and consistent. The new effort must be communicated and discussed actively, in meetings, on the phone, and by email. In fact, a regular flow of communication about the new initiative is one of the keys to implementing it successfully.

Here is how to implement this accountability:

- Use "The One-Page Sales Planner" discussed in Chapter 35.

- Have your sales leader specify how many actions, and which ones, he would like that week. For example, this week, give us five did you know questions, five referral requests, and five quote follow-ups. You may have different actions for different departments. Customer service takes incoming calls all day. So you might focus on did you know questions and reverse did you know questions for them, which they can easily drop into existing phone calls. That's 15 actions. That's three per day. Which is approximately one minute of additional activity per person per day. That's one minute, executed by everyone, day after day, that turns into millions of dollars in new sales.

- Ask for customer-facing staff—that's inside sales, outside sales, customer service, and anybody else who interfaces with customers—to create a plan and track their results. If the plan was to ask a did you know question today, ask for the following details in the results: Did you ask? *Who* did you ask? Which customer (company and name)? What product did you ask about? And how did the customer respond? You can do all of this in two sentences next to each did you know: *Asked Tom at Widgets Inc. about our WX298. He did not know, and is dissatisfied with current provider. We are sending samples.*

- Make sure everyone knows that it must be turned in to his or her manager by the end of the week. Before people finish working on Friday, they should finish up their planner, fill out any remaining details, and send it in to their manager.

- The managers should give feedback on this planner to people individually, copying executive leadership.

- If somebody doesn't turn in a planner, communicate with that person. *What happened? I thought we were on the same page.*
- It's okay to use words like *mandatory*. It must be clear that this is a permanent initiative. *This* sales change must be different from all the others.

Long-term change must be focused on the long term. If you concentrate on it for only two months, your people will look away as soon as you do. Think of yourself as the personal trainer for this initiative.

Corporate change is like a new exercise program: many times, when people miss the first workout, the entire program ends. They simply don't return. Diets are the same way: one bad meal or weekend often kills a diet. Don't let one bad meal kill your company's new initiative. Keep it in front of the staff, regularly and consistently, for a long time.

Talk about it internally. Use the language. Let people get used to hearing the terminology.

Recognize the successes—publicly. Studies find that recognition among peers is a far more effective motivator than financial compensation. That is, one proactive company-wide compliment is more powerful encouragement than a $1,000 bonus, or even a $10,000 bonus. Why? Because it's public, and it makes the recipient proud.

It also allows peers to witness, and learn from, the person's successes. Those same peers will now aspire to be recognized next. So we benefit from the psychology of people not wanting to miss out on the next opportunity for recognition. By publicly recognizing one person's success, you benefit from improved action throughout much of your organization. Executive leaders should send an email to everyone identifying top results, and recognizing top performers.

Finally, a steady stream of positivity flies around your company when you recognize success regularly. This is tremendously useful for behavioral change. It makes people want to participate, which is far more effective than change that is demanded.

Recognize those lagging behind—publicly. That's right, along with complimenting proactively, don't be afraid to call people out who are simply choosing not to participate. Of course, speak to them privately first, but if that doesn't help, do it in a departmental meeting or by email to the entire group.

The key is that this recognition of poor participation occurs in the same communication in which you address the successful implementers. Don't communicate the stick without the carrot. We need both. Positivity is the major theme in this work. Usually, being called out once like this is enough. People will do everything they can to never be in the "lagging" group again.

Wider efforts are more successful. Some of my clients have only the owner or CEO handling the implementation. That is, the same person communicates the activities for the week, gives feedback on the planners, identifies and distributes the recognition, and also speaks privately to the people whose participation isn't up to standards. Oh, and this person also runs the company. It's too much for one person. It's not surprising, then, that those companies that have more managers involved in the implementation of this work do better than those that have just one. I talk to these leaders separately from everybody else in our projects, teaching them how to implement accountability and drive this process within their groups. It's train-the-trainer work.

A wider effort is more successful because more people own the outcome. More people implement accountability. And they are closer to their staff than the top executive. They're on the battlefield with their team daily, rather than in the rear, on horseback, directing strategy. It's also easier for the owner or CEO to interact directly with a few key leaders, driving their approach to management, than every front-line person doing this work.

The Two Greatest Differentiators between My Clients Who Grow the Most, and Those Who Grow the Least

All of my clients add to their growth rate when they do this work.

Nobody has done this work and grown *less,* which is basically impossible if customers and prospects are hearing from you exponentially more.

But some clients grow much more than others. Some grow by 30 percent in their first year, while others grow by 5 percent.

What's the difference?

My examination of this arrived at two critical factors. These are the two most important differentiators between my clients who grow the most and those who grow the least. And like most determinants of corporate success, they start with the owner or top executive.

The Leaders Who Implement Accountability the Best Grow the Most

The most successful growers have leaders who say, "Where is it? You said you would do this. What happened?"

The most successful creators of change are experts at accountability.

They seek to gain commitments to new efforts, and when somebody doesn't do something they committed to, the executive asks why not?

They spend time talking to their managers, helping them hold their teams accountable.

They make it clear that this is an important initiative and that everybody is expected to participate.

They don't say, "Try it."

They say, "I expected you to do this."

They don't say, "I hope you give this a shot."

They say, "This is mandatory."

There's no shame in this.

You keep your promises. Employees are paid every two weeks, just as you committed to them. You're accountable to that.

And they must be accountable to you.

The Companies That Talk About This the Most Grow the Most

The second (of two) top determinant of success with this work is, "Does it become a part of the culture?"

Does it become a part of the conversation inside your company?

Do you talk about it?

Do you meet about it?

Is it on the walls?

The companies that talk about this the most are the companies that grow the most.

And here's the key: it needs to be more than just one person communicating to the front-line staff. The top performers feature the communications flowing in both directions, from many of the various people who are involved in the work.

For example, a customer service person sends an email to everybody detailing how she asked for a referral and received one, and detailing what it might be worth to the business.

Her colleagues reply to her, and congratulate her on her success, while being reminded of (or learning) a technique they can also try.

Her immediate supervisor replies to all and offers some more details.

Then the owner or CEO hits reply all and congratulates her on the effort.

Similar exchanges occur in meetings.

What does this kind of active communications do? Why does it cause success?

1. It shows people that their peers and colleagues are actively engaged in the work and *enjoying great success.*

2. More simply, it reminds people to do the work.

3. It's clear this is important to the owner or the CEO. You're involved. You're present. You're giving this attention. You're giving *your people* attention as it relates to what is important to you.

4. The positive interactions and congratulations provide encouragement and enthusiasm for the effort. It's fuel.

5. People see that this works. Consistently. This is no small thing. It brings those people who are on the fence along. It allows you to say, "We know this works here, and I need your involvement in growing this business."

6. The recognition makes those being recognized proud and happy, but it also makes the others, who are *not* being recognized, *aspire* to be next. They will strive for your recognition going forward.

7. People begin to speak a common language. The vocabulary becomes consistent. *"I asked an rDYK and then pivoted to the sale three different ways, and they added it to their order!"*

The power of accountability and consistent attention infuses a new effort into your culture.

And when the revenue-growing techniques laid out here become one with your culture, you will find your business adding at least 20 percent annually to its sales.

And *that* is a beautiful thing.

To discuss implementing this Selling Boldly process for your organization, call me at 847-459-6322, or email me at alex@goldfayn.com.

37 | Now, Go Help More People More

Now you know.

You know the critical mindsets that are required to quickly and easily sell more.

You know exactly what proactive communications to implement with your customers *and* prospects, and you know what to say or write when you make them.

You know precisely what to do now, don't you?

But you kind of knew before you started reading, didn't you?

You know this stuff.

The difference between today and every other day is that today you start doing *what you know you should be* doing.

Today we begin doing the work repeatedly and systematically, day after day, a few seconds at a time.

Today we begin going about the work of helping our customers more.

Today we begin to help more people more.

Because that's all sales growth is.

Helping more people more.

And you're really good at helping people.

Go do what you're great at.

Help your customers and prospects.

And they'll thank you with their money.

You deserve it.

Acknowledgments

I usually thank my wife, Lisa, at the end of this section, building up to my most important person and all, but I'm going to start with her here. She handles literally *everything* in our home and family so that I can do this work, and she does so with grace, elegance, and nary a negative word. On top of that, she supports me without doubt or question, and, more than once over our 20 years together, she has been more confident and secure about my work than I was. Without her, I simply would not be capable of doing this work. None of it.

This book is dedicated to my incredible eight-year-old twins, Bella and Noah. They are my reason for working, and traveling all over the world for clients and events, and helping people as hard and as much as I can. They are my why. When I don't feel like it, I think about them, and then I do it. It's easy then.

As everyone who has seen me speak in the last three or four years knows, my parents brought me here to the United States from the former Soviet Union, where there was little chance and less hope, when I was two years old. They took incredible risks and showed astounding courage to come here for a better life, mostly for me. I am grateful for their strength every day.

I'd like to also thank Lisa's parents, Ron and Jan Lobodzinski, and my brother-in-law, Keith Lobodzinski, for their support and love over the years. My grandmother Bella, a young and independent 91 years old at the time of publication, offered much-needed support when I was struggling to find my way in business 15 years ago or so, and she brings it up to me frequently now. "Your grandma told you that you'll be just fine, and *I was right!*" Grandma is always right.

I have friends in the consulting business who teach, listen, commiserate, and support me as the years go by. They are Colleen Francis, Chris Patterson, Jeff Conroy, and, there for both shallow and deep conversations nearly daily is my best friend in the business, Wes Trochlil. He received updates on the progress of this book from me daily, whether he wanted them or not.

My assistant, Jenna Jessup, does the urgent detail-oriented work in my practice so that I can help as many clients as possible. I am grateful for her daily efforts and organization. She is very good at that—me, not so much.

I need to say thank you to my wonderful clients. First I want to thank Pete Traeger, Mark Fisher, and Ryan Hillsinger for allowing me to use some of our project tools and data in this book. I'm very grateful for your support and belief. Also high on the list of clients to thank: Karl Hallstrom, Brian Gale, Matthew Turco, Howard Halderman, Michael Gianni, Tom Leddo, Josh Hudson, Adam Hudson, Martha Flannery, Mike Meiresonne, Paul Kennedy, Gary Pieringer, Brent Bernardi, Frank Rotello, and Phil Sperling. I consider you friends first and clients second.

Thanks to Kathy Pierce for an 11th hour review of this manuscript.

Finally, to the good people at John Wiley & Sons, starting with my editor and friend, Richard Narramore: he has gone to bat for me multiple times, and I came to him with this idea first. He didn't let me go anywhere else. Thank you, Richard. It's always a joy to work with you. Thanks also to Shannon Vargo, Danielle Serpica, Peter Knox, and Sharmila Srinivasan for your hard work.

Appendix: 100 Questions to Ask Your Customers and Prospects (and Yourself)

Headline: 100 Revenue Growth Questions

The more we communicate with customers and prospects, the more we sell.

The more that people hear from us, the more they buy from us.

(The opposite is also true: the less they hear from us, the less they buy.)

We are not bothering them.

We are not disturbing them, or taking their time. No.

Rather, we are helping them.

We are letting them know we care.

We care more than the competition does.

We are thinking about them.

We are here for them. The competition isn't. But we are.

And so, we must systematically communicate this to our customers and prospects.

Regularly and consistently communicate helpfully with your customers.

If possible, make these communications automatically. Personally, but automatically.

My entire Revenue Growth Habit process, which I implement for my clients, is based on this. My clients simply out-communicate the competition. The day this revenue growth program launches, my clients' customers and prospects hear from them exponentially more than before.

And nobody complains about receiving too many communications because these are *helpful* communications, useful to the recipient.

Most of the communications in my system of revenue growth are questions.

I teach the customer-facing people at my clients' companies to ask these questions regularly and systematically.

We track the questions, and critically, the outcomes. What did you ask or do, and what happened? What were the results?

Then, we measure the outcomes. That is, we asked for 61 referrals this week, received 40 (two-thirds is the typical return-on-referral request that my clients enjoy). We followed up with all of these referrals, connected with 30 of them, and closed 10. These new customers average approximately $45,000 in orders over the course of a year, creating a $450,000 ROI on *one week's worth of referrals,* each of which takes 30 seconds to one minute to ask for.

It gets better: there are 50 more such weeks to repeat! And, there are 40 or so additional techniques in my revenue growth system.

Because most of the communications in my approach to revenue growth are questions, here are 100 questions you can ask yourself and *your customers and prospects* to grow your sales.

First, Some Questions to Ask Yourself

First, here is a series of questions to ask yourself, your executive leadership, your salespeople, your customer service people, and anyone who faces and interacts with customers.

1. How do I help my customers and prospects? (If you don't know, ask them. They'll tell you.)

2. Do I *know* how good I am? Do I have an awareness of it?

3. Is my material—website, brochures, and *even personal emails*—about my products and services, or about how I help my customers?

4. Do I focus on how I help my customers and prospects, or on my stuff? When my customers talk about my material, they talk about my value. I need to think and talk more like my customers.

5. Do I communicate proactively or reactively? If I am like most people, I spend my time reacting to customer issues, but revenue growth is a proactive pursuit.

6. Am I bold or modest? Revenue growth is no place for modesty.

7. Am I optimistic or pessimistic? The research shows that optimistic salespeople outperform pessimistic ones every time, by a lot.

8. Do I persevere always or do I give up easily? The research of the great Martin Seligman shows that perseverance and resilience are twice as important as talent.

9. Am I grateful—for these customers, these prospects, this wonderful company, and these excellent products and services that really help people—or am I cynical, focused on the negative? Grateful salespeople are proven to outperform cynical ones.

10. Am I asking for the business every time it is discussed? Am I pivoting to the sale at every opportunity?

11. Because my customers can *feel* my attitude, am I bold, confident, and positively *on* during every sales conversation?

Questions for Your Customers and Prospects

There's one simple key about these questions. They are best asked on the phone or face to face. Person to person. Their return, impact, and value goes way down if communicated by email. Nearly all of them can be asked during existing conversations you're already having, meaning these revenue-generating questions take just seconds—*moments*—to ask.

You don't need to ask all of these questions. Just ask some, here and there, but consistently throughout your day.

To Increase Sales per Customer

The typical customer has conscious awareness of just 20 percent of what you can offer them. Which means they're buying what you can help them with elsewhere. Ask these questions to increase this awareness percentage:

12. Did you know we also do x?

13. Are you aware we do y?

14. Most people don't know we do z. Do you have a minute to talk about it?

15. What percent of your business on this product or service would you guess we have? How do we increase that by 10 or 20 percent? (It's a small increase for your customer, but for you it adds up in a hurry across 10 or 20 customers.)

16. Do you need some of these or that?

17. Most of our customers who buy this also add these three items. Shall we add them to your order also?

18. What are you buying elsewhere that I may be able to help with?

19. You know, we have a customer in a similar company to yours, and they buy products x, y, and z. I know you have a need for these too. May I add some to your next order?

20. I'd like to work with you more. What would that look like?

21. We still have some room in your box/truck/rail car. Should we fill it with product x or y?

22. What are you working on these days that I can help with?

23. Just checking in. How are you? What's new?

To Get Testimonials

Your customers speak and think more positively about you than you speak about yourself. Your customers are happy. And you need to know this. No, you need to *marinate* in this! And then you need to share their happiness with other customers and prospects!

24. What are some of your favorite things about working with us?

25. Why did you say that?

26. Remind me. How long have we been working together?

27. That's a long time; what's kept you with us so long?

28. How does working with me help you?

29. What specifically gets better when we work together?

30. Does working with us save you time?

31. How much time, approximately?

32. Do you think working with us saves you money?

33. That's interesting. Tell me about that.

34. Why?

35. *How much* money would you guess you save with us?

36. Do we help you *make* money?

37. How so?

38. Do we help you look good to your customers?

39. How?

40. How many suppliers do you have in all?

41. If you were to rank us on the kinds of things we're talking about now, from best to worst, where do you position us among that group?

42. If you were describing us to a peer or colleague who does not know us, what would you say?

43. What are the first three emotional words that come to your mind when you think about working with us?

44. Is it okay with you if we use some of your comments in our materials? (This is the only permission question that you need. Nearly everyone will say yes.)

Note: None of the preceding questions mention the word *testimonial,* which is stressful and uncomfortable. You're just asking people for their feedback. Just like having a drink with a friend.

To Use Testimonials

There are passive ways to use testimonials—that is, posting them on your website, in your materials, on your walls—and active ones, which involve communicating them one on one. These questions deal with this kind of active communication. These are about *selling* with testimonials.

45. We have a customer similar to you. May I show you what they have to say about us?

46. Here's a customer buying a different kind of product (or service) from us than you are. And here is what they have to say about us. I'd like to bring this kind of value to you. Is it better for you to connect on Tuesday or Thursday?

47. Here's what some customers like you have to say about us. Now can I help you this way, too?

48. Our clients tell us we save them approximately 20 percent of their time compared to working with our competition. I'd like to help you this way.

49. Let's talk about doing this for you. When should we connect?

50. Here are three customers who say we've grown their sales by at least 20 percent. Now, how about we discuss doing this for you?

51. Our customers tell us they consider us a partner, not a vendor. We'd like to be *your* partner. When is a good time to discuss this?

52. Check out this amazing testimonial that we just got. [Read or show testimonial.] Want to talk about doing this here?

To Ask for Referrals

We are so uncomfortable with asking for referrals. But our customers are not. Our customers LOVE giving referrals. Why? Because they get to help twice—a friend or colleague, and us. In turn, it makes them look good in the eyes of their friend and they look good to us. And finally, it gives them leverage. If they need something from us, we will work hard to help them. People love giving referrals. We just need to ask for them.

53. Who do you know like yourself who would benefit from working with me like you do?

54. What colleagues do you work with at your company who I can help like I help you? I'd like to help your company more.

55. What suppliers do you work with who I can help like I'm helping you? I'd like to make you look good.

56. What about customers? Who buys from you who I can help like I've helped you?

57. I work with owners or purchasing managers or heads of sales. Who do you know like this?

58. What groups are you involved with where you or your peers gather? Who do you know there whom I can work with like you and I work together?

59. I enjoy working with you a lot. Who do you know who I'd enjoy working with as much as I enjoy working with you?

60. We met each other through a referral. It's how I grow my business and feed my family. Now it's your turn. Who do you know like yourself who'd benefit from working with me like you do?

Once you get a name, do not stop. Establish concrete next steps. Ask the question and wait for an answer! Do not talk into the silence.

61. Do you prefer that I reach out to him or her and use your name, or would you like to connect us?

62. I appreciate you doing that. When do you think you'll get to it so that I don't jump the gun?

63. *Summarize:* Okay, so you'll let him know I'm calling next week, and I'll wait until Thursday and then reach out. Sound good?

Note: I don't mention the word "referral" in any of these. That's another stressful word. Furthermore, the key to actually getting an answer to these questions is *silence*. Ask the question; then stop talking and listen. Do not speak first. Let the person think and answer your question. *You've* been thinking about asking for this referral for a long time, but your customer has not!

To Ask for the Business

Too often, we do everything but ask for the business, and the customer does not buy. Avoiding the pivot to the sale has to do with our fear of rejection. The customer is talking to us. They want our help. We would like to help them. And so, we must ask for the business. Ask everyone you talk to about your products and services. If it's not time to ask for the business, pivot to the next yes. Ask one or more of these questions until you get the business.

64. Shall we write it up?

65. Would you like to add to this order, or shall we write it up separately?

66. Cash or credit?

67. We have that in stock. Shall we get it out in today's shipments?

68. It looks like we have only one (or a few) left. Want it?

69. Will you be writing a check or financing it?

70. Sound good?

71. How many would you like?

72. I have eight in stock. Do you want them all?

73. We've had a lot of interest in those. Would you like to lock them?

74. I can have it to you tomorrow. Ready to go?

75. Would you like to add product x or y to this order?

76. Do you want to send me a purchase order or should we just put it together now?

77. Which location would you like me to ship it to?

78. Want to increase that to six units and save $25 per unit?

79. Any questions before I enter your order?

80. When should I expect payment?

Note: Once again, the key here is silence. Ask and wait. Don't talk first. Let the customer think. They're adults; tell them you're interested in their business, in helping them, and then let them answer your question.

To Follow Up on Quotes and Proposals

When there is no response to a quote or proposal your customer requested, follow up with these three questions. Send them in succession, with an appropriate amount of time (depending on your deal and the customer's timing) in between.

81. Did you get the quote I sent yesterday after we talked? These things tend to get picked off by spam filters.... Let me know if it got to you.

82. It's been a few days and I haven't heard from you about the quote I sent. Where are you at on this?

83. Just one final check-in on that quote we discussed, as you haven't responded to my follow-ups. I want to make sure I'm not dropping the ball on this. Do you still want it? Please let me know within 24 hours, because the quote is expiring very soon.

To Check In Proactively by Phone

How many one-on-one proactive phone calls do you get? Most people get almost none. A proactive· call is different from a call when you need something. Check in with your customers and prospects. Be present. Be helpful.

84. I was just thinking about you. What are you working on these days?

85. We were just talking about you, and I wanted to pick up the phone. How are you?

86. Your name came up recently, and it reminded me to reach out. What's happening in your world? What can I help you with?

87. You know, we didn't come together on that thing we talked about last year but I was thinking about you and wanted to check in. How are you doing on that thing now?

88. We didn't come together last quarter (or month or week or day), but where are you at on it now?

89. How's business?

90. How's your family?

91. What's the latest in your world?

To Follow Up after Delivery or Conclusion of Work

92. Just checking in. Did everything arrive okay?

93. Are you happy?

94. Do you need anything else?

[AND . . . pivot to another question . . .]

95. Great! Who do you know like yourself who would enjoy working with us like you do?

96. Excellent! How much of your business would you guess we have?

97. I'm very glad now. What else are you buying elsewhere that I may be able to help you with?

And the Three Most Important Questions, from Me to You

Now that you know exactly what to ask and how to ask it:

98. Who will you ask?

99. What will you ask?

100. What will you do?

Ask these questions throughout your day. They don't have to be exactly these questions, either. Make them your own. And, in fact, own them. Then enjoy all the additional sales that you generate!

Index